EDITORIAL RESEARCH REPORTS ON

The
Women's Movement

ACHIEVEMENTS AND EFFECTS

Timely Reports to Keep
Journalists, Scholars and the Public
Abreast of Developing Issues, Events and Trends

Published by Congressional Quarterly Inc.

**1414 22nd Street N.W.
Washington, D.C. 20037**

About the Cover

Cover design by Howard Chapman, art director of Editorial Research Reports.

PRINTED IN THE UNITED STATES OF AMERICA, JUNE 1977

Editor, Hoyt Gimlin
Editorial Assistants, Barbara Cornell, Diane Huffman
Production Manager, I. D. Fuller
Assistant Production Manager, Maceo Mayo

Library of Congress Cataloging in Publication Data

Editorial research reports on the women's movement: Achievements and Effects

Bibliography.
Includes index.
1. Feminism—United States—Addresses, essays, lectures. 2. Sex discrimination against women—United States—Addresses, essays, lectures. I. Congressional Quarterly, Inc. II. Title: The women's movement.
HQ1426.E36   301.41'2'0973   77-9245
ISBN 0-87187-115-7

Contents

Foreword

When Editorial Research Reports published a book four years ago titled *The Women's Movement,* we found it safe to say that "the movement has refused to fade into oblivion and become merely a passing fad on the American scene." The staying power of the quest for women's equality in the home and the work place, and in society at large, had already become apparent. Now after the passage of four years we are attempting to assess some of the movement's achievements and effects in this compilation of reports that have been issued since the first book was printed.

These achievements and effects cannot be toted up neatly into win-loss columns or plotted on pieces of graph paper. But we hope that from the information here provided, the reader may discern the relative strength or weakness of the women's movement in several areas where it is manifest, notably in the home and on the job. Men and women's roles in both places are being redefined, Sandra Stencel writes in this book's opening report, "The Changing American Family." Whether in response to changing views of their role in society or from economic necessity—or both—women are entering the labor market at an unprecedented rate. More than half of the women above age 19 work outside the home.

The redefining of the women's role in society is having a profound effect upon family life. This is reflected not just in the weighty pronouncements of psychologists and sociologists, but in the rising divorce rate and the sinking birth rate. Rapidly changing values are creating doubts and uncertainties in parents and children. Traditional notions of morals and propriety are being challenged and defied. How will it all end? The experts cannot agree whether the family will prevail in its traditional mode or whether it will finally disintegrate, or perhaps be permanently reshaped by forces acting upon it.

Many of these forces—the primary ones—are given expression in the women's movement and in some cases have been set in motion by the movement. Professor Edward Shorter of the University of Toronto ventures that we are seeing a revolution that is no less important to everyday people than the great industrial revolution of the last century. Only time will tell, but just the achievements and effects chronicled in this book suggest that the movement is bringing about changes that were undreamed of in its infancy.

Hoyt Gimlin
Editor

June 1977
Washington, D.C.

THE CHANGING AMERICAN FAMILY

by

Sandra Stencel

June 3
1977

THE CHANGING AMERICAN FAMILY

J OHN AND MARY Smith are getting a divorce. Smith's frequent business trips and long work hours were a source of friction. Despite his frequent absences, he was upset when his wife announced that she was going back to work, especially when she said it would mean that Grandpa Smith would have to go to a nursing home. Tensions in the Smith household increased when their oldest daughter got divorced and moved back home with her two young boys. Then the youngest daughter left home to live with her boyfriend. And just recently, the son dropped out of college and joined a religious commune.

This fictional family may sound like it sprang from the script for "Mary Hartman, Mary Hartman." But similar scenarios are being played out in millions of real households across the nation. Caught in the middle of broad social and economic changes, American families are finding it increasingly difficult to cope with their problems. Rapidly changing values are creating uncertainties and doubts in parents and children. Traditional notions of parental authority and responsibility are being questioned. Old taboos on sexual conduct in and out of marriage are breaking down. Men and women's roles in the home and in the work force are being redefined.

In the face of all these changes, observed Alan Pifer, president of the Carnegie Corporation, "important governmental and private-sector policies that intimately affect the family...are still in the main geared to earlier value systems and beliefs. Social policies have not yet caught up with changing social practice."[1] Evidence of stress in the family is not hard to find.

The divorce rate in the United States is the highest in the world. Nearly 40 per cent of all marriages now end in divorce. Census Bureau statistics show that the U.S. divorce rate more than double between 1963 and 1975 *(see table, p. 5).*[2]

Over 11 million children—more than one out of six children under age 18—live in single-parent homes. Since 1960, the number of such families has grown seven times as fast as the number of two-parent families.[3]

---

[1] Alan Pifer, "Women Working: Toward a New Society," *1976 Annual Report of the Carnegie Corporation of New York.*
[2] Bureau of the Census, "Marital Status and Living Arrangements: March 1976," *Current Population Reports,* Series P-20, No. 306, January 1977, p. 2.
[3] See "Single-Parent Families," *E.R.R.,* 1976 Vol. II, pp. 661-680.

The number of marriages performed in the United States declined about 7 per cent from 1973 to 1975, according to a 1976 study by the National Center for Health Statistics. On the other hand, the number of couples living together out of wedlock more than doubled between 1970 and 1975. Today approximately 1.3 million unmarried Americans share living quarters with a member of the opposite sex, the Census Bureau calculates.

"The change in family life under way today," declared Edward Shorter, professor of history at the University of Toronto, "is of no less magnitude, and will have no less importance in the lives of common, everyday people than did the great industrial revolution of the last century."[4]

Conflicting Views Over Family Stability

Experts agree that the family as an institution is facing many new challenges. But they are divided on the question of how well the family is meeting them. Some, like Drs. Urie Bronfenbrenner of Cornell University and Amitai Etzioni of Columbia University, point to the rising divorce rate, declining marriage and fertility rates, and rising numbers of women leaving home for paid work as symbols of the deterioration of the American family. "At the present accelerating rate of depletion, the United States will run out of families not long after it runs out of oil," Etzioni wrote recently in *Science* magazine.[5]

Etzioni and Bronfenbrenner's concerns are shared by President Carter. In a campaign speech last August in Manchester, N.H., Carter said: "[T]he breakdown of the American family has reached extremely dangerous proportions." He pledged that his administration would do everything in its power to reverse this trend *(see p. 15)*. Shortly after taking office, Carter urged his staff members not to neglect their family responsibilities despite job pressures. He admonished federal workers to marry rather than join the growing ranks of couples "living in sin."

Bruno Bettelheim, director emeritus of the Orthogenic School at the University of Chicago, has said that the most serious problem facing today's family is "the discrepancy between its present reality and expectations of what it ought to be." In his opinion these expectations are completely unrealistic and antiquated. "The false expectation is that today's family should function as well as families in the past," he wrote. "The fact is that the conditions which gave substance to the earlier family and made for its cohesion...are no longer present."[6]

---

[4] Edward Shorter, "Changing from Nuclear Nest to Intimate Couple," *Journal of Current Social Issues*, winter 1977, p. 10. The *Journal* is published by the United Church of Christ.

[5] Amitai Etzioni, "Science and the Future of the Family," *Science*, April 29, 1977, p. 487. Etzioni is professor of sociology at Columbia and director of the Center for Policy Research. Bronfenbrenner is professor of human development and family studies at Cornell.

[6] Bruno Bettelheim, "Untying the Family," *The Center Magazine*, September-October 1976, p. 5.

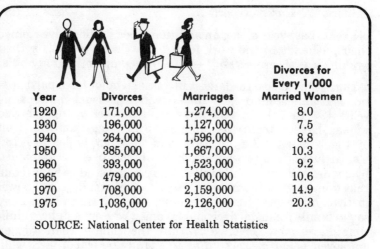

Year	Divorces	Marriages	Divorces for Every 1,000 Married Women
1920	171,000	1,274,000	8.0
1930	196,000	1,127,000	7.5
1940	264,000	1,596,000	8.8
1950	385,000	1,667,000	10.3
1960	393,000	1,523,000	9.2
1965	479,000	1,800,000	10.6
1970	708,000	2,159,000	14.9
1975	1,036,000	2,126,000	20.3

SOURCE: National Center for Health Statistics

A different view of today's family was presented by Mary Jo Bane, a professor at Wellesley College, in her book *Here to Stay: American Families in the Twentieth Century* (1976). She concluded that American families are as strong as ever. Many of the trends in family life which Bronfenbrenner, Etzioni and others found disturbing were, she thought, positive changes. Professor Bane found notions of the good old days romanticized; those happy extended families of assorted relatives living under one roof, as portrayed in Norman Rockwell paintings, were rare. "The nuclear family, consisting of parents living with their own children and no other adults, has been the predominant family form in America since the earliest period on which historians have data," she wrote.[7]

Bane argued that what divorce is doing to disrupt families today, death did in earlier times. In fact, she said, the proportion of children affected by "parental disruption" actually has declined over the last century. Even with the rising divorce rate, more children today are living with at least one parent than ever before. One reason for this is the large increase in the proportion of widowed and divorced women who continue living with their children after their marriage has ended rather than sending the children to live with grandparents, other relatives or to orphanages. While the high rate of divorce in the United States is cause for concern, she said, the high rate of remarriage indicates that marriage "is still a pervasive and enduring institution."

The Implications of Women's Employment

In recent years American families have undergone a fundamental change in the manner in which they provide for their economic welfare. Since 1950, the number of families in which both husband and wife work has climbed from 22 per cent to 42

---

[7] Mary Jo Bane, *Here to Stay: American Families in the Twentieth Century* (1976), p. 37. Bane is associate director of Wellesley's Center for Research on Women.

per cent. Last year alone, an additional one million wives joined their husbands in the work force.[8] The prime reason for their working was sheer necessity—to help keep up with family bills.

During the 1950s, the largest increase in labor force participation was among married women beyond the usual childbearing years (20 to 34). In recent years, however, young married women have entered the labor force in large numbers. Half of the working wives in 1975 had children under age 18.[9] The arrival of the two-paycheck family has been accompanied by a redefinition of family roles. A number of studies have found that women who are employed exercise a greater degree of power in their marriages. Most especially, working wives have more say in family financial decisions. Women who are employed full-time have more leverage within the family than women employed part-time, according to a study by Isabel V. Sawhill and Kristin A. Moore of the Urban Institute in Washington.[10]

Closely related to the issue of marital power is the question of how the employment of women affects the division of labor within the home. Sawhill and Moore found that "in general, husbands of working wives engage in slightly more child care and housework than do husbands of nonworking women." But they go on to say that "it does not appear that the rapid movement of women into the labor force has been matched by any significant increase in husbands' willingness to help around the house."[11]

Although most husbands welcome the additional income, many have found it difficult to adjust to their wives' new roles. Being married to a woman with a busy schedule, an income of her own, and outside friendships and commitments may cause a husband to feel insecure and resentful. Numerous studies have shown that there is more divorce among families in which the wife works.[12] Once society has adjusted to women's new roles the divorce rate might decline somewhat. But, according to Sawhill and Moore, "if the economic achievements of women continue to undermine the utilitarian character of traditional marriages, a permanently higher rate of divorce is a likely outcome."

Changing Attitudes Toward Child-Rearing

Today's families are not as child-oriented as they were in the 1950s. Many parents have come to believe that they are entitled to pursue their own interests—even if it means devoting less

---

[8] See "Women in the Work Force," *E.R.R.*, 1977 Vol. I, pp. 121-144. See also Howard Hayghe, "Families and the Rise of Working Wives—An Overview," *Monthly Labor Review*, May 1976, p. 16.

[9] U.S. Department of Labor, "U.S. Working Women: A Chartbook," 1975.

[10] Kristin A. Moore and Isabel V. Sawhill, "Implications of Women's Employment for Home and Family Life," The Urban Institute, August 1975, pp. 7-8.

[11] *Ibid.*

[12] See Heather L. Ross and Isabel V. Sawhill, *Time of Transition: The Growth of Families Headed by Women*, 1975, pp. 35-66.

Perhaps no one is a better symbol of today's changing values and life-styles than is Ms. Joanie Caucus, the plucky 42-year-old divorcee from Gary Trudeau's daily comic strip "Doonesbury." For the past three years some 60 million readers have followed her bittersweet metamorphosis from runaway wife and mother to day-care center supervisor, law school applicant and student, and live-in lover of hip Washington journalist Rick Redfern. The culmination of Joanie's search for herself came on May 21, when she and her 225 real-life classmates received their diplomas from the law school at the University of California at Berkeley.

time to their children and making fewer sacrifices for them. In return, they expect less from their children later on. These were the findings of a recent survey of parents of children under 13 years of age conducted by Yankelovich, Skelly and White, the national market research and public opinion organization, for the General Mills Consumer Center.[13]

Two out of three parents interviewed for the General Mills survey said that parents should have their own lives and interests even if it means spending less time with their children; 54 per cent said that people have no right to count on their children to help them when they are old or in difficulty; 67 per cent said that children have no obligation regardless of what parents have done for them; and two out of three do not believe a couple should stay married just for the sake of the children.

The emphasis on self-fulfillment was greatest in the group identified by Yankelovich as the "new breed" parents. The "new breed," representing 43 per cent of the parents interviewed, tend to be better educated and more affluent. They stress freedom over authority, self-fulfillment over material success, and duty to self over duty to others—including their own children. The study found that "new breed" parents are loving but take a *laissez-faire* attitude toward child-rearing. "It's not the permissiveness of the '50s," said Yankelovich, "which was child-centered and concerned with the fragility of the child. Today, the parent says in effect, 'I want to be free, so why shouldn't my children be free?' "[14]

---

[13] "Raising Children in a Changing Society, The General Mills American Family Report 1976-77."

[14] Quoted in *Time*, May 2, 1977, p. 76.

By contrast, the traditionalists, who still represent the majority of parents (57 per cent of those interviewed), are stricter disciplinarians, more demanding of their children and more willing to make sacrifices for them. But Yankelovich found that not even the traditionalists are prepared for the same kind of self-sacrificing approach to child-raising that was common in their parents' time. For example, a solid majority of the traditional parents (64 per cent) agreed that (1) parents should have lives of their own even if it means spending less time with their children, (2) parents should not stay together for the sake of the children, and (3) children have no obligation to their parents regardless of what parents have done for them.

Many social scientists fear that the emphasis on individualism and self-gratification throughout the culture—which author Peter Marin has labeled "the new narcissism"[15]—is harming the family. Another writer saw the family "being destroyed by the egocentricity of each member."[16] Professor Etzioni expanded on this theme. "People must learn to balance the personal rewards of 'doing one's own thing' against the hurt it might entail to others," he wrote. "No relationships, no institution, family or society can survive otherwise."[17]

Rise in Number of Childless Marriages

Some contend that the new narcissism is responsible for the growing number of young married couples who have decided not to have children—ever. In 1955, according to statistics compiled by the Census Bureau, only 1 per cent of all wives between the ages of 18 and 24 expected to have no children. By 1973, that figure had risen to 4 per cent. Today it stands at 5 per cent.[18] Since 1957, the fertility rate *(see explanation, p. 19)* in the United States has dropped from 3.76 children per woman to 1.75 last year. Philosopher Michael Novak has written that the notion of family is so unpopular these days that a decision to have children, formerly a routine event in a young married couple's life, now requires "an act of courage."[19] Disillusionment with parenthood seems particularly strong among college students.

The adage that "having children can bring a couple closer together" has been displaced by statistics showing that child-rearing puts a severe strain on marriage. Separate studies by Dr. Harold Feldman, professor of human development and family studies at Cornell University, and Dr. Charles Figley, a research

[15] Peter Marin, "The New Narcissism," *Harper's*, October 1975, p. 45.
[16] Abram Kardiner quoted in *Human Behavior*, May 1977, p. 73.
[17] Amitai Etzioni, "The Family: Is It Obsolete?" *Journal of Current Social Issues*, winter 1977, p. 8.
[18] Bureau of the Census, Current Population Reports, Series P-20, No. 248, p. 19; No. 265, p. 19; and No. 277, p. 17.
[19] Michael Novak, "The Family Out of Favor," *Harper's*, April 1976, p. 37.

Black Families In the United States

The troubles of black families gained much attention in 1965 with the publication of the so-called Moynihan Report. Prepared by the Department of Labor's Office of Policy Planning and Research under the direction of Daniel P. Moynihan, then an Assistant Secretary of Labor, the controversial report argued that the black family was "deteriorating" because women headed about one-fourth of these families. The report also noted that nearly a quarter of urban Negro marriages were dissolved and nearly one-quarter of Negro births were illegitimate. This breakdown of the black family structure, the report said, had led to a "startling increase" in welfare dependency.

Black families continue to suffer from higher rates of dissolution than white families. In 1975, 10 per cent of all persons of ages 25 to 54 who had ever married were either divorced or separated; the corresponding figures for whites and blacks were 8 per cent and 27 per cent, respectively. Only 49.4 per cent of the black children were living in households with both parents present, compared with 85.4 per cent of the white children. Children in black families were three and a half times more likely to be living below the official poverty level as were white children.

There have been some signs of improvement among black middle-class families. A recent study of social mobility by two University of Wisconsin sociologists, Robert M. Hauser and David L. Featherman, found a vast improvement in the black family's ability to pass on to its sons the social advantages it had managed to acquire. In the early 1960s, it did not matter very much whether the family was poor or middle class—the son usually had to start on the bottom rung of the job ladder. By the early 1970s, however, he was much more apt to start out at, or rise to, the status level of his father, and his career was more apt to reflect the advantages bestowed by his parents.

psychologist and marriage counselor at Purdue University, found that generally the sense of satisfaction with the marriage does drop during the child-raising period. A team of researchers at the University of Michigan's Institute for Social Research found that married childless couples were the happiest group in society.

One of the greatest burdens of child-rearing is financial. The U.S. Commission on Population Growth and the American Future reported in 1972 that the average cost of rearing a child to age 18 was $35,000.[20] Today the figure is much higher. The U.S. Department of Agriculture estimated in 1975 that the yearly expense amounted to 15 to 17 per cent of family income. This meant that a family earning between $16,000 and $18,000 a year would spend nearly $50,000 on a child during his or her first 18 years. College costs would add another $20,000.

---

[20] *Population and the American Future: The Report of the Commission on Population Growth and the American Future,* March 1972.

9

A new study by the Population Reference Bureau[21] stated that the average cost of rearing and educating a child in the United States ranged from $44,000 for relatively low-income families (earning $10,000 to $13,500 a year after taxes) to $64,-000 for middle-income families ($16,500 to $20,000). What's more, these figures represented only direct costs. Adding in the "lost" earnings of mothers who stayed home to care for young children boosted the average costs to $77,000 for low-income families and $107,000 for middle-income families.

Married couples who choose to remain childless still are a small minority. Most who choose this route complain that it is a tough decision to make because of pressures from friends, neighbors and, most of all, parents who want to be grand-parents. And there is indirect pressure—the glorified picture of parenthood presented by the press, television, movies and advertisements. The National Organization for Non-Parents (NON), headquartered in Baltimore, Md., was founded in 1972 to fight this cultural bias against childless couples and to challenge the pro-natalist pressures in society. NON's founder, Ellen Peck, emphasized that the group is not against parenthood—just against the social pressures that pushed people into having children whether or not they really wanted them.

NON also supports the growing number of couples who are choosing to have only one child. In 1975, approximately 11 per cent of all wives aged 18 to 39 said they wanted a one-child fami-ly as compared to only 6 per cent in 1967. Various experts have attacked the image of the only child as spoiled, selfish, lonely and isolated. The organization quotes Dr. Murray M. Kappelman, professor of pediatrics at the University of Maryland, as saying: "...[T]here is absolutely no reason why the only child cannot be as emotionally sound and as socially stable as every other well-adjusted child on the block."[22]

Diminishing Influence of Parents on Teens

The high divorce rate and the increase in the number of people postponing or foregoing marriage and child-rearing are not the only signs of families under stress. Incidents of violence within the family have jumped sharply in recent years. According to estimates supplied to the Department of Health, Education and Welfare by the American Humane Association, one million children are the object of neglect or abuse each year, and 2,000 to 4,000 die from circumstances involving neglect or

---

[21] Thomas J. Espenshade, "The Value and Cost of Children," *Population Bulletin,* April 1977.
[22] "The One-Child Family," brochure published by the National Organization for Non-Parents.

abuse.[23] According to authors Roger Langley and Richard C. Levy, 28 million American women are "battered wives."[24]

Urie Bronfenbrenner contends that the deterioration of American family life is responsible for the plight of today's youth. Teenage alcoholism and drug abuse are growing problems.[25] The suicide rate for young people 15 to 19 years old more than tripled in the last two decades, climbing from 2.3 per 100,000 in 1956 to 7.1 per 100,000 in 1974. Recently there has been an increase in suicides among younger children, some as young as ten.[26] Crimes by youths under 18 years old have been growing at a higher rate than has the juvenile population. Bronfenbrenner estimates that children are running away from home at the rate of one million a year. He and other social scientists are concerned about the diminishing influence of parents on children and the growing importance of peer group relations and television. "What we are seeing here...are the roots of alienation...."[27]

Christopher Lasch, professor of history at the University of Rochester, argues that the laissez-faire attitude of today's parents toward their children may be responsible for the growing number of youngsters who are turning to Rev. Sun Myung Moon's Unification Church, the Hare Krishnas and other religious cults. "The ease with which children escape emotional entanglements with the older generation leaves them with a feeling not of liberation but of inner emptiness," Lasch wrote recently. "Young people today often reproach their parents with indifference or neglect, and many of them seek warmth and security in submission to spiritual healers, gurus, and prophets of political or psychic transformation."[28]

Bruno Bettelheim has suggested that increased tension between parents and their adolescent children in recent years is the unavoidable consequence of the extension of the age of dependency. Until a few generations ago, he pointed out, most children left home at the beginning of puberty to join the labor force. "It is something entirely new that most children are kept economically—hence also socially—dependent on their parents until they are twenty or older," he wrote.[29]

---

[23] See "Child Abuse," *E.R.R.*, 1976 Vol. I, pp. 65-84.

[24] Roger Langley and Richard C. Levy, *Wife Beating: The Silent Crisis* (1977).

[25] See "Resurgence of Alcoholism," *E.R.R.*, 1973 Vol. II, pp. 987-1007, and Richard C. Schroeder's *The Politics of Drugs* (1975).

[26] Figures cited by Urie Bronfenbrenner in "The Disturbing Changes in the American Family," *Search*, fall 1976. *Search* is published by the State University of New York.

[27] Urie Bronfenbrenner, "The Isolated Generations," *Human Ecology Report*, winter 1976, p. 7.

[28] Christopher Lasch, "The Undermining of the Family's Capacity to Provide for Itself: How Mass Education and Madison Avenue have Replaced Main Street and Mommy and Daddy," published in *The Washington Post*, Feb. 10, 1977.

[29] Bruno Bettelheim, *op. cit.*, p. 9.

Historic Forces and Home Life

FAMILY LIFE in early America was shaped in large part by older European traditions. The colonies retained the patriarchal family patterns and the strict Judeo-Christian sexual codes of their European ancestors. "On the other hand," wrote Professor William M. Kephart of the University of Pennsylvania, "certain circumstances in early America operated to bring about changes in the European family system."[30] For one thing, there was a marked shortage of women. Consequently, women had much choice in the selection of a husband and the dowry system became obsolete. Frontier conditions also favored relative independence for the young.

Households in colonial America generally were larger than in Europe. It was common for a family to have from five to ten children, and 15 or more was by no means rare. Benjamin Franklin, for example, came from a family of 17. But contrary to popular mythology, the extended family household, populated by an assortment of related people of all ages, was never the dominant family form in America. The first U.S. census in 1790 showed the average size of a household was 5.8 people.

The early colonial family tended to be a farm family and thus an economically self-sufficient unit. Although the women occasionally assisted with the heavier duties, tasks generally were divided along sex lines, with the men doing the land clearing and construction and the women doing the cooking and food processing, spinning and weaving, washing and mending and candle-making. Children were expected to assist their parents. Farm tools were both scarce and crude, and the farmer needed all the help he could get. Children were economic assets.

Marriage was considered an obligation as well as a privilege. People were expected to marry, and they normally did so at a young age, girls often in their early teens and boys frequently before they were 20. "There was little place in colonial society for the unmarried...," Kephart wrote. "For a woman, marriage was deemed to be the only honorable state.... Bachelors were suspect, and in most of the colonies were heavily taxed and kept under close surveillance.... Widows and widowers were expected to remarry and they did, usually without much time elapsing."[31]

The position of women and children in colonial America was only slightly better than in Europe. In New England, especially, where the social milieu was heavily patriarchal, wives and children faced severe social and legal restraints. However,

---

[30] William M. Kephart, *The Family, Society, and the Individual*, 2nd ed. (1966), p. 120.
[31] *Ibid.*, pp. 191-192.

women were accorded certain legal rights and protection. Husbands were responsible for the support of their wives and for any debts incurred by them. Women had inheritance rights with regard to their husbands' property. Additionally, wives were legally protected against any abuse or maltreatment by their husbands. Strict discipline and parental respect were the hallmarks of child-rearing practices.

Divorce was exceedingly rare. Plymouth—settled in 1620—did not experience a divorce until 1661. In some of the colonies, particularly in the South, there were simply no provisions for divorce. In colonies that did make provisions, the legal grounds were usually confined to adultery or cruelty and often were punishable as criminal offenses. In many of the colonies, the legislatures rather than the courts were empowered to pass on divorce requests.[32]

Liberalization of Courtship and Sex Mores

There were no real changes in the status of American women until late in the 19th century. As late as 1850, a wife had no legal control over her own personal property; all her belongings were legally in the hands of her husband, to dispose of as he saw fit. Her services also belonged to him, and she had no legal rights even to the custody of her own children. Women were not permitted to vote, nor was their education taken very seriously. Female wage earners were looked upon with suspicion. "In general," concluded Professor Kephart, "a woman had little alternative but to marry and fulfill her 'child-bearing and homemaking destiny.' "[33]

The rights of women were gradually broadened under the impetus of the women's rights movement launched in 1848 at a convention in Seneca Falls, N.Y.[34] Eventually women won the right to vote, to negotiate contracts, run their own businesses, keep their own earnings, and to attend institutions of higher learning. Women began entering the work force in increasing numbers. The first large-scale influx of women workers took place in the New England factories of the mid-19th century. During the Civil war more occupations were opened to women, a phenomenon that was to be repeated in World War I and World War II. By 1900 women comprised 18 per cent of the work force.

The folkways and mores of courtship also changed. From the colonial period to the Civil War, the changes were slow, but thereafter, the tempo increased. The use of dowries ceased altogether. Parental permission to begin courtship was no longer

---

[32] Edmund S. Morgan, *The Puritan Family* (1944).
[33] Kephart, *op. cit.*, p. 25.
[34] The Woman's Rights Convention at Seneca Falls is generally cited as the beginning of the woman's suffrage movement, the forerunner of today's women's movement. See "Status of Women," *E.R.R.*, 1970 Vol. II, pp. 582-583.

a strict necessity. While parents still had a fair measure of control over the marriages of their sons and daughters, love matches were growing in favor. A rapidly increasing urban population meant that single people had more leeway in the choice of mates. Urbanization was accompanied by an increase in commercial amusements—theater, athletic events and public dances. "Opportunities for meeting young people of the opposite sex were so widespread...that a new term was coined: dating.[35]

As the 20th century dawned, the same forces that tended to liberalize courtship—emancipation of women, accelerated urbanization, decline in secular and religious controls—served to weaken the existing sex mores. Three additional factors were (1) automobiles, (2) increased availability of contraceptive devices, and (3) a relatively simple treatment for venereal disease. There is general agreement that after World War I there was a substantial increase in premarital petting, premarital intercourse and adultery. Equally important were the changes in attitudes toward sex. The biggest change was that marital intercourse came to be regarded as an activity which was pleasurable for the wife as well as the husband.

There were no nationwide divorce statistics in the United States until the mid-19th century. The very absence of such figures suggests that divorce was rather infrequent. In 1867, the Census Bureau counted 9,937 divorces among the 37 million people in the United States. By 1900, the population had roughly doubled, while the yearly number of divorces had increased to 55,751. By 1950, the population had again doubled, but during that year divorces had soared to 385,144. As the divorce rate increased over the decades, the stigma attached to divorce tended to decline.

Along with changes in courtship, sex behavior, marriage and divorce came striking changes in the functions of the American family. "In the colonial era," Kephart wrote, "the family...was not only economically independent but also served as the center for such activities as education, religion and recreation.... With the disappearance of the frontier, however, together with rapid increases in urbanization and industrialization, traditional family functions were taken over by...institutions or agencies."

Impact of Depression and World War II

Economic and social forces have had a significant impact on family structure in the past 50 years. During the depression years of the 1930s, the average age at marriage rose sharply, and 9 per cent of the women had not married by age 50. Birth rates plummeted. Lifetime childlessness approached 20 per

---

[35] Kephart, *op. cit.*, p. 237.

cent, and many of the children whom some demographers thought were merely being postponed were never born. One explanation for this, according to Census Bureau demographer Paul C. Glick, "is that many of the women who delayed having those other children reached the point where they liked it better without them than they had thought they would."[36]

World War II caused extensive dislocations in family life, particularly among families with husbands—or would-be husbands—of draft age. Marriage and birth rates remained low, and millions of women, married as well as single, were welcomed into the work force. The proportion of women in the labor force reached 36 per cent during the war, and then dropped sharply to 28 per cent with the return of the veterans to civilian jobs.

The postwar period was marked by a sharp, brief increase in marriage and divorce rates, but both quickly fell back down. The mid-1950s were, in Glick's words, "a relatively familistic period." Much emphasis was placed on family-oriented activities. Popular culture, especially the new medium of television, glorified the happy American home. Couples married younger than before, and all but 4 per cent of the women married during their childbearing years. The baby boom that had started with the return of the World War II servicemen reached its peak in 1957; 4.3 million babies were born in the United States that year. The birth rate did not diminish significantly until after 1960. By that time the rate of entry into marriage had already begun to fall and the divorce rate had resumed its long upward trend.

National Family Policy Proposals

THERE CAN BE NO "more urgent priority for the next administration," Jimmy Carter said in his campaign speech in Manchester, N.H., "than to see that every decision our government makes is designed to honor and support and strengthen the American family." Carter repeated this theme in his Inaugural Address: "I...hope that when my time as your President has ended, people might say...that we have strengthened the American family, which is the basis of our society...." To this end, President Carter will convene a White House Conference on Families in 1979. A prime purpose of the conference will be to examine the ways government policies affect family life.

[36] Paul C. Glick, "Some Recent Changes in American Families," *Current Population Reports*, Special Studies, Series P-23, No. 52, p. 1.

Sidney Johnson, director of the Family Impact Seminar at George Washington University, will coordinate the White House Conference. Johnson also has been assigned the task of advising all Cabinet departments on ways to be more responsive to the needs and concerns of families. For example, Secretary of Defense Harold Brown will weigh family considerations as part of a coming review of the military's policy of transferring career personnel to different posts every two or three years.

Many organizations and individuals have urged the federal government to develop and adopt a coherent national family policy. Urie Bronfenbrenner said in a recent interview: "The United States is now the only developed country in the world that doesn't have a national program providing child care for working parents, minimum family income, and health care for families with young children.... What's destroying the family isn't the family itself but the indifference of the rest of society."[37]

Fragmentation of Government Programs

One of the leading proponents of a national family policy is Vice President Walter F. Mondale, who, as senator, was chairman of the Subcommittee on Children and Youth. "We need to begin shaping a society that doesn't just tolerate family life or pretend to be neutral toward it," he wrote recently. "We need instead a society that nourishes it and helps it grow."[38] Mondale has said that while the United States has no formal policy, this does not mean that the nation has no family policy at all. "What we have," he wrote, "might best be called a family policy 'by default'—a series of largely unexamined, unarticulated, and largely inconsistent, burdensome policies with respect to families."[39] As examples of government policies that create hardships for families, Mondale cited frequent transfers of military and foreign service personnel and welfare regulations that deny federal AFDC—Aid to Families With Dependent Children—payments to families unless or until the father leaves home.

Mondale has suggested that the United States test the feasibility of developing "family impact statements"—similar to the environmental impact statements that are now required by federal law. "I believe the family impact idea holds great promise," he said, "but I also believe its political, administrative, and substantive feasibility must be carefully tested.... Clearly we do not need a family protection agency or bureaucracies ensuring impact statements on all proposed

[37] Interview in *Psychology Today*, May 1977, p. 41.
[38] Walter Mondale, "The Family in Trouble," *Psychology Today*, May 1977, p. 39.
[39] Walter Mondale, "Government Policy, Stress and the Family," *Journal of Home Economics*, November 1976, p. 13.

policies or laws.... What we do need instead is to test the idea of a family impact statement on several public policies in a purely advisory fashion. We need to start a public conversation about the impact of legislation on families."

The key to preserving the family, in Bronfenbrenner's opinion, is to require changes in the workplace. He advocates (1) flexible work schedules that allow parents to be home when their children come home from school, (2) fair part-time employment opportunities that do not deprive the worker of fringe benefits, status and seniority, (3) sick leave for working parents when children are ill, and (4) paternity leave as well as maternity leave. Such policy changes will have to be accompanied by changes in attitudes. Americans will have to discard the notion that domestic considerations should give way before the demands of the job. These policy changes also will require more cooperation between men and women in the sharing of family responsibilities.

Many social scientists have advocated creation of an income support system for families. Their proposals include a "negative" income tax, a system of family allowances, or a combination of the two. Nearly all of them contemplate elimination of the present program of aid to families with dependent children. Professor Bane goes a step further and suggests that a form of Social Security be devised to cover the first 20 years of a person's life, those of greatest dependency. The person would repay this amount during his or her working years. Bane conceded that there would be enormous difficulty in establishing such a plan. For one thing, the costs would probably be enormous.

Opponents of family allowances are concerned with more than just the cost. They fear that such a system would lead to public intrusion into child-rearing practices. They also worry about the tendency of such systems to encourage people to have more children. Another argument is that childless people should not be asked to subsidize people who choose to have children.

Visions of Future of Marriage and Family

Bane thinks that family commitments are likely to survive in society because "it seems clear [that they] are not archaic remnants of a disappearing traditionalism, but persisting manifestations of human needs for stability, continuity and non-conditional affection." Her optimistic assessment of the future of the family draws general agreement. But there also seems to be general agreement that the definition of the family needs to be broadened to include not only the nuclear family but also single-parent families, communal families, childless families, homosexual couples, and others. Robert Hill, director

17

of research for the National Urban League, has said: "We must stop confusing the structure or form of family life with the capacity of families to function."[40] Along these lines, the Department of Housing and Urban Development recently announced that it was opening public housing to unmarried couples living together and to homosexual couples if they could show a "stable family relationship."

The wide range of existing family patterns in the United States was disclosed in the following statistics:[41] Three groups—childless couples, couples whose children are grown and households headed by women—now represent nearly a quarter of all family groups; another quarter falls into such categories as communes, affiliated monogamous families sharing a common household, unmarried couples, single persons alone, single persons living together for economic or convenience reasons without forming a true "family," and stable homosexual couples. Finally, 4 per cent of the families still are reported to be "extended," those in which grandparents or such other relatives as uncles or aunts are part of the household. This means that fewer than half of all American families fall into the category of a traditional nuclear family—father, mother and children living together in their own household.

According to Professor Edward Shorter, the "couple-family" will be the predominant family type of the future. The couple-family will differ from the old nuclear family in several ways. There will be fewer children, and those children will have less influence on their parents' emotional lives. The man-woman relationships will be based on a high level of sexual attraction and a desire for intimacy, and consequently the couple-family will be more socially isolated from the rest of the community, be it neighbors, friends or colleagues from work. And because of this sexual intensity, "the couple-family is going to develop the pattern of coming together, revelling for a few years in intense intimacy, then breaking apart again," Shorter wrote.[42]

Predictions of Another U.S. Baby Boom

Some see a different future for the family. Several demographers have predicted that the nation is on the verge of a new baby boom. University of Michigan demographer Ronald Lee has predicted that fertility will start to rise around 1980, increase steadily through the mid-1980s, and peak in the 1990s with women once again bearing an average of more than three children apiece. Lee and other like-minded demographers base their predictions on a perceived relationship between birth

---

[40] Quoted by Joseph Giordano and Irving M. Levine in "Carter's Family Policy: The Pluralist's Challenge," *Journal of Current Social Issues,* winter 1977, p. 51.

[41] Cited by Marvin Sussman, "An Immodest Proposal," *The National Elementary Principal,* May-June 1976, p. 35.

[42] Shorter, *op. cit.,* p. 13.

cohorts—the number of people born in any particular year—and earning power. Demographer Richard Easterlin, professor of economics at the University of Pennsylvania and father of today's most accepted baby boom theory, described the relationship in its application to procreation:

> One of the factors that seem to have been important in the last baby boom was the relative [small] number of young people in the labor market.... These people then had lots of children—the baby boom cohorts—so that in the sixties and seventies there was a relative glut of young people on the market and they've had a somewhat rough time.
>
> They had fewer children than their parents had had, and now some of their children—the first of the post-baby-boom cohorts—will soon be entering the labor market. And when they do, there are going to be relatively few of them and they are going to find themselves relatively well off, and thus the baby trend is going to swing upward again.[43]

Recent statistics give some validity to the new baby boom theory. The latest figures from the National Center for Health Statistics show a slight increase in the general fertility rate, which measures the number of births per 1,000 women of childbearing years. The seasonally adjusted general fertility rate rose to 68.3 during January 1977, the highest it had been since October 1974 when it was 69.8. It was 65.1 in January 1976. Two other measurements of the country's childbearing also increased. The birthrate—which measures the number of births per 1,000 population, including everyone of every age, not just women—and the number of live births both increased about 1 per cent in the 12 months ending in January 1977. Population experts said the statistics gave some indication that women in their late twenties and early thirties may be deciding not to put off childbearing any longer.

If a new baby boom does come, it will not necessarily mean a return to the values of the fifties. Women are unlikely again to turn to motherhood as a full-time occupation. Nor will they continue to assume the full burden of childbearing. Women are unlikely to have more children unless men are willing to assume equal responsibility for their care and society is willing to provide adequate family support systems.

[43] Quoted by Linda Wolfe in "The Coming Baby Boom," *New York*, Jan. 10, 1977, p. 40. See also Carl L. Larter's "The 'Good Times' Cohort of the 1930s," *PRB Report*, April 1977. *PRB Report* is published by Population Reference Bureau Inc., Washington, D.C.

Selected Bibliography

Books

Bane, Mary Jo, *Here To Stay: American Families in the Twentieth Century*, Basic Books, 1976.
Kay, F. George, *The Family in Transition*, John Wiley & Sons, 1972.
Kephart, William M., *The Family, Society, and the Individual*, Houghton Mifflin, 1966.
Shorter, Edward, *The Making of the Modern Family*, Basic Books, 1975.
The Women's Movement, Editorial Research Reports, 1973.
Yorburg, Betty, *The Changing Family*, Columbia University Press, 1973.

Articles

Bettelheim, Bruno, "Untying the Family," *The Center Magazine*, September-October 1976.
Bronfenbrenner, Urie, "The Disturbing Changes in the American Family," *Search*, fall 1976.
Hayghe, Howard, "Families and the Rise of Working Wives—An Overview," *Monthly Labor Review*, May 1976.
Journal of Current Social Issues, winter 1977 issue.
Kron, Joan, "The Dual Career Dilemma," *New York*, Oct. 25, 1976.
Mondale, Walter F., "Government Policy, Stress, and the Family," *Journal of Home Economics*, November 1976.
——"The Family in Trouble," *Psychology Today*, May 1977.
Novak, Michael, "The Family Out of Favor," *Harper's*, April 1976.
"The American Family: Can It Survive Today's Shocks," *U.S. News & World Report*, Oct. 27, 1975.
Ware, Ciji, "Is A Baby Worth the Price?" *New West*, April 25, 1977.
Wolfe, Linda, "The Coming Baby Boom," *New York*, Jan. 10, 1977.

Reports and Studies

Editorial Research Reports, "Marriage: Changing Institution," 1971 Vol. II, p. 759; "Single-Parent Families," 1976 Vol. II, p. 661; "Women in the Work Force," 1977 Vol. I, p. 121.
Espenshade, Thomas J., "The Value and Cost of Children," *Population Bulletin*, April 1977.
Glick, Paul C., "Some Recent Changes in American Families," *Current Population Reports*, Special Studies, Series P-23, No. 52, 1975.
Moore, Kristin and Isabel V. Sawhill, "Implications of Women's Employment For Home and Family Life," The Urban Institute, August 1975.
Pifer, Alan, "Women Working: Toward a New Society," *1976 Annual Report of the Carnegie Corporation of New York*.
"Raising Children in a Changing Society, The General Mills American Family Report 1976-77."
U.S. Bureau of the Census, "Fertility History and Prospects of American Women: June 1975," *Current Population Reports*, Series P-20, No. 288, January 1976.
——"Marital Status and Living Arrangements: March 1976," *Current Population Reports*, Series P-20, No. 306, January 1977.

WOMEN IN THE WORK FORCE

by

Sandra Stencel

**Feb. 18
1977**

WOMEN IN THE WORK FORCE

RESPONDING TO changing views of their role in society and inflationary pressures on family budgets, women are surging into the U.S. labor force at an unprecedented rate. Not even in the World War II days of Rosie the Riveter did so many women work outside the home. Nearly half—47 per cent—of the American women 16 and older held jobs or were actively looking for work last year. Among women aged 20 to 64, the prime working year, the percentage was even higher. Over 56 per cent of the women in this group were employed.[1]

The number of American women who work has been rising steadily since 1947 *(see box, p. 25)*. But during the last few years and especially in 1976, women entered the job market at a pace called "extraordinary" by Alan Greenspan, chairman of President Ford's Council of Economic Advisers.[2] Last year 1.6 million women entered the work force. Over the past 25 years the number of American working women more than doubled, rising to nearly 39 million in 1976 from just 19 million in 1951. The Bureau of Labor Statistics estimates that nearly 12 million more women will be added to the work force by 1990.[3] According to the same projection, the number of men in the labor force will grow by less than 10 million during that period. Although men are expected to continue to make up the larger part of the labor force, their participation is expected to continue its slow, long-term decline.

The Department of Labor, in its "1975 Handbook on Women Workers," labeled this increase in the number and proportion of women who work as "one of the most spectacular changes in the American economy in the past quarter-century." Eli Ginzberg, a Columbia University economist and chairman of the National Commission for Manpower Policy, called it "the single most outstanding phenomenon of our century," and he went on to say that "its long-range implications are absolutely unchartable."[4]

Some economists say that the influx of women—and also teenagers—into the labor force accounts for the nation's con-

[1] Statistics from U.S. Department of Labor, Bureau of Labor Statistics, "Employment and Earnings," Vol. 23, No. 5, November 1976, pp. 21-22.
[2] White House press conference, Sept. 3, 1976.
[3] *Monthly Labor Review*, October 1976, p. 2. The *Monthly Labor Review* is published by the Department of Labor.
[4] Quoted in *The New York Times*, Sept. 12, 1976.

tinued high unemployment rate. In 1976, the nation's unemployment rate fluctuated between 7.3 and 8.1. For both adult
men and women, the rate was lower, but for teenagers it was far
higher, as the following table illustrates:

Period	Overall Rate	Adult Women*	Adult Men*	Teen-agers
1976	7.7%	7.4%	5.9%	19.0%
1975	8.5	8.0	6.7	19.9
1974	5.6	5.5	3.8	16.0

* 20 and older

The primary cause of the current unemployment rate has not
been people losing their jobs, John O'Riley of *The Wall Street
Journal* wrote, but rather "the unprecedented number of new
job seekers scrambling to get on the paycheck bandwagon."
Time magazine commented that "the profound consequence" of
women and teenagers entering the job market in large numbers
"is that the number of people looking for work is leaping faster
than the economy can provide jobs...."[5]

Feminists contend that such arguments ignore the economic
reasons which force most women to seek work. "The only
justification for those who, for political advantage, try to blame
our high unemployment rate primarily on the spectacular influx
of women into the labor force is that at least they have pin-
pointed a profound change in the labor force," wrote financial
columnist Sylvia Porter last September. "Their argument is
viciously sexist. Their explanation shrugs off the vital importance of the woman's paycheck to prosperity and to the standard of living of millions of households."[6]

Economic and Social Factors in the Upsurge

Like all complex social changes, the back-to-work movement
has been shaped by many economic and cultural forces.
Economic need is clearly one of them. "Women now work
because they have to," said Arlene Kaplan Daniels, a
Northwestern University sociologist. This was especially true for
the 8.5 million single women in the labor force in 1975 and for
the nearly seven million women workers who were divorced or
separated from their husbands. Of all women in the work force,
about one out of eight (12.3 per cent) was either divorced or
separated, according to a recent report by Allyson Sherman
Grossman, an economist with the Bureau of Labor Statistics.[7]

[5] *The Wall Street Journal*, Jan. 17, 1977, and *Time*, Nov. 1, 1976, p. 25.
[6] Sylvia Porter, writing in *The Washington Star*, Sept. 20, 1976.
[7] Allyson Sherman Grossman, "The Labor Force Patterns of Divorced and Separated
Women," *Monthly Labor Review*, January 1977, pp. 48-53. Daniels was quoted in
Newsweek, Dec. 6, 1976, p. 69.

Women in the Work Force

Year	Number (add 000)	Percentage of Adult Female Population*
1947	16,683	31.8
1951	19,054	34.7
1956	21,495	36.9
1961	23,838	38.1
1966	27,333	40.3
1971	32,132	43.4
1972	33,320	43.9
1973	34,561	44.7
1974	35,892	45.7
1975	37,087	46.4
1976	38,520	47.4

*Ages 16 and older

Source: U.S. Department of Labor

Economic need was also behind the sharp rise in the labor force participation of married women in recent years. Of the more than 21 million married women who were in the labor force in March 1975, approximately 26 per cent were married to men earning less than $10,000 a year. Nearly three million working women had husbands who were unemployed or unable to work.[8] As inflation has eroded real disposable income, many middle-class families have come to rely on wives' earnings to maintain their standard of living. Without a second paycheck, they would find it difficult—if not impossible—to buy a house or send their children to college.

A number of factors other than economic need and the rising divorce rate have contributed to the increased number of working women. These include: (1) more effective means of birth control and the trend toward fewer children; (2) the increased life expectancy of women; (3) the greater number of college-educated women; and (4) the widespread use of labor-saving devices in the home. Other factors are the expansion of the white-collar job market in which most women are employed, the increase in part-time employment opportunities, and legal action prohibiting job discrimination based on sex.

There has been a tremendous change in attitude toward working women in recent years, primarily as a result of publicity given to the woman's movement. "As recently as 10 years ago, a woman had to defend her position if she wanted to work," said Beatrice Buckley, editor of a new monthly magazine called

---

[8] U.S. Department of Labor, "Why Women Work," July 1976.

Working Woman. "Now you have only to go out and ask the nearest housewife what she does and she'll answer, 'Just a housewife.' "[9] A recent survey of teenage girls and young women conducted for the American Council of Life Insurance found that only one in four wanted to be a housewife.[10]

A Roper Poll for *Fortune* in 1936 indicated that only 15 per cent of the population believed "married women should have a full-time job outside the house." Another Roper Poll for the magazine 10 years later found that by a 5-3 ratio Americans thought that housewives had more interesting lives than women who held full-time jobs. By 1969 the national temper had changed, according to a Gallup Poll. By a 5-4 majority, the poll's respondents said there was nothing wrong with married women earning money in business and industry.

A Gallup Poll in March 1976 found that 68 per cent of those interviewed approved of working wives. A study conducted later in the year by *The Washington Post* and the Harvard University Center for International Affairs indicated that men favored careers for women by a 2-1 ratio, women by 4 to 3. However, a nationwide poll conducted by Research Analysis Corp. of Boston for *Newsday* found that nearly half of those it surveyed agreed with the statement, "If a man doesn't want his wife to take a job, she should respect his wishes."[11]

Widening Pay Gap Between Men and Women

Women's pay has increased significantly in recent years but not as fast as men's *(see graph, p. 27)*. Consequently the difference between men's and women's pay is wider today than it was 20 years ago, according to a report issued last October by the Women's Bureau of the Department of Labor titled "The Earnings Gap Between Women and Men." It also noted that women earned substantially less than men at the same level of education. In fact, the average woman college graduate earned less than the average male high school drop-out. The study found that women were overrepresented at the lower end of the pay scale as the following table illustrates:

Earning Group	Male	Female
$ 3,000-$4,999	36.6%	63.4%
5,000-6,999	41.9	58.1
7,000-9,999	59.3	40.7
10,000-14,999	83.1	16.9
15,000 and over	94.7	5.3

---

[9] Quoted in *Newsweek*, Dec. 6, 1976, p. 69.
[10] American Council of Life Insurance, "The Family Economist," Nov. 3, 1976.
[11] *Post*-Harvard poll appeared in *The Washington Post*, Sept. 28, 1976, and the Research Analysis Corp. poll in *Newsday*, June 15, 1976.

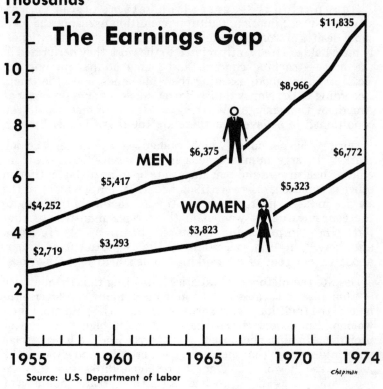

MEDIAN EARNINGS
Thousands

The Earnings Gap

MEN

$4,252
$2,719
$3,293
$5,417
$6,375
$3,823
WOMEN
$5,323
$8,966
$11,835
$6,772

12

10

8

6

4

2

1955   1960   1965   1970   1974

Source: U.S. Department of Labor

chapman

The widening wage gap between the sexes reflects the continued concentration of women in relatively low-skilled, low-paying jobs. According to the Department of Labor's "1975 Handbook on Women Workers," more than two-fifths of all women workers were employed in just 10 job categories in 1973: secretary, retail sales worker, bookkeeper, private household worker, elementary school teacher, waitress, typist, cashier, sewer and sticher, and registered nurse. Salaries were relatively low, averaging $4,700 for sales clerks and $6,400 for clerical workers. More than one-third of all women workers were employed in clerical jobs.

Helping to fill the clerical ranks are many college-educated women who cannot find other work. The Equal Employment Opportunity Commission estimates that 20 per cent of the college graduates who work are in clerical, semi-clerical or unskilled jobs. Economists say this is partly because many women major in the liberal arts and enter the job market with few marketable skills and partly because of discrimination. Businesses still tend to groom male college graduates for management jobs and women graduates for the secretarial pool.

Occupational segregation stems from many sources—discrimination, cultural conditioning, and the personal desires of women themselves. The jobs women traditionally have held are frequently related to the work they performed in the home—teaching children and young adults, nursing the sick, preparing food, assisting their husbands and other men. According to Dr. Nancy Smith Barret, an economics professor at American University in Washington, D.C., women have been conditioned to believe that these are the only "proper" jobs.[12]

During the period in which women were entering the job market in large numbers, jobs in the service industries, including health care and teaching, were opening up faster than in other occupations. Between 1964 and 1974, employment in the service industry nearly doubled. Another factor contributing to the concentration of women in the service industries is that part-time employment is more obtainable there than elsewhere.[13] In 1974, according to the Department of Labor, about 28 per cent of all working women held part-time jobs.

Despite the plethora of statistics indicating that the majority of women work because of economic need, many employers still hold to the traditional view that men ought to be paid more than women. Employers reason that men merit higher salaries or preference in hiring because they will not withdraw for marriage and childbearing; that men can give more time and effort to the job because they have no domestic responsibilities; that they are more valuable as employees because of their greater mobility; or that they need more money to support their families. Because they see women as temporary fixtures in the labor force many employers tend to shuttle women into jobs where the skills are quickly learned and there is little opportunity for advancement.

"The threat of discontinuity in a woman's worklife is perhaps the greatest single barrier to higher wages for young women," the new Secretary of Commerce, Juanita Kreps, wrote in her book *Sex in the Marketplace: American Women at Work* (1971). She added:

> The period of heaviest domestic responsibility occurs fairly early in a woman's worklife, when she is likely to be forced to make some quite long-range decisions: whether to acquire further job training, or additional formal education; how many children she will have; whether to continue working, at least part-time, during the childbearing period.... Her immediate job choice is dictated in large measure by the time constraint imposed in the short-run, and this choice in turn directs her subsequent career development.

---

[12] Quoted in *Redbook*, March 1975, p. 88.
[13] See article by Elizabeth Waldman and Beverly J. McEaddy, "Where Women Work—An Analysis by Industry and Occupation," *Monthly Labor Review*, May 1974, p. 3.

Because of their family responsibilities, many women prefer jobs that require little or no overtime work or traveling. One of the attractions of elementary school teaching for women is that they can coordinate their work with their children's schedules.

Shift to Professional and Blue-Collar Jobs

The pay gap does not disappear when women go into the professions. The median income for women college professors is 91 per cent that of their male colleagues. The average salary for women high school teachers is 81 per cent that of men. Female scientists earn 76 per cent as much as male scientists, and female engineers 85 per cent as much as their male counterparts. In some professions the situation for women is getting worse, not better. The latest figures from the National Center for Education Statistics in the Department of Health, Education and Welfare show that during the 1975-76 school year, the average salary for male faculty members rose faster than for females.

Almost 16 per cent of all women in the U.S. labor force are in the professions, mostly nursing and teaching. But growing numbers are seeking fuller access to such traditionally male-dominated professions as law, medicine, architecture, business and engineering. Today about 23 per cent of all law students in the United States are women, up from 8.5 per cent in 1971. The number of first-year women medical students has more than doubled since 1972.[14] About 25 per cent of all entering medical students are women, up from 11.3 per cent in 1970 and 8.9 per cent in 1965.

Among the nation's 1,300 biggest companies, *Business Week* reported Jan. 10, 1977, there are about 400 women directors versus about 20 just five years ago. However, these 400 represent only 2.7 per cent of the 15,000 board members of major corporations. More and more women are becoming junior executives and sales representatives, positions that often lead to the top. International Business Machines, which employed 400 women sales representatives in 1973, now has 1,400. At Xerox the percentage of women in the sales force has grown to 14.9, up from 1.7 in 1971. In other fields, too, women are starting to move up through the ranks. A recent report on commercial banking by the New York-based Council on Economic Priorities showed women making significant gains in managerial, professional, technical and sales posts.[15]

[14] See Mary Lynn M. Luy, "Status Report on Women in Medical Education: Up and Coming," *Modern Medicine*, Nov. 1, 1976, p. 33. The American Bar Association figure of 23 per cent is limited to women enrolled in ABA-approved law schools.

[15] The council found that between 1971 and 1975 the percentage of all bank managers and officials who were women jumped from 16 to 26. The number of women in professional, technical and sales categories climbed from 22 to 35 per cent. However, only 13 per cent of the bank officers and 1.8 per cent of the senior executives were women.

Women have made some inroads into blue-collar jobs that up until recently have been largely male enclaves. The signs of change are everywhere. From 1962 to 1975 the ratio of men to women changed from 70-1 to 20-1 among garage workers and gas station attendants, from 35-1 to 11-1 among mail carriers, and from 27-1 to 11-1 among taxicab drivers.[16] In Seattle, an organization called Mechanica has placed women as carpenters, machinists, diesel mechanics, laborers and truck drivers. Over 3,000 women were employed on the Trans-Alaska Oil Pipeline as craftsmen, clerks and cooks. Approximately 11,000 women make their living as carpenters and 700 women as coal miners.[17]

Despite these gains, the number of women who have cracked the sex barriers is relatively small, and the sight of women at the bottom of mines, at the top of telephone poles, and in the ranks of the police, firefighters and the military academies still draws the attention of the public and the news media. The Department of Labor, in its latest report on the subject, said that only 18 per cent of the total number of blue-collar workers were women at the end of 1975, about five million women in all.

History of Working Women in U.S.A.

V ERY FEW PEOPLE know that the official version of the Declaration of Independence, the one that was circulated to all the colonies, was printed by a woman—Mary Katherine Goddard of Baltimore. "The job of printing the Declaration went to a woman," author Caroline Bird wrote, "because as publisher of the leading newspaper in town, she had the facilities to do it."[18] In addition to being a successful newspaper publisher and printer, Mary Katherine Goddard was the new nation's first, and for many years the only, woman postmaster.

Although Mary Goddard was not typical of the women of her time, she was not unique either. Many colonial women were employed in the trades. Since most work was done at or near home, wives often assisted their husbands and frequently carried on the business if they were widowed. Many had come to the colonies as indentured servants and worked as domestic servants during their bondage. Other colonial women (especially

[16] Figures from Peter A. Morrison and Judith A. Wheeler, "Working Women and 'Woman's Work': A Demographic Perspective on the Breakdown of Sex Roles," The Rand Corporation, June 1976, p. 2.

[17] The Kentucky Commission on Human Rights has ordered a number of coal companies in the state to hire more women and wants women eventually to fill 20 per cent of the mining jobs in Kentucky. See *United Mine Workers Journal*, January 1977, p. 13.

[18] Caroline Bird, *Enterprising Women* (1976), p. 6.

widows) kept inns and taverns, managed retail businesses, and became seamstresses and milliners. The most important occupations for women during this period were spinning and weaving. At first most of this work was done at home. But as the demand for textiles increased, the factory system developed. By 1850, the textile mills of New England employed some 92,000 workers, two-thirds of them women.[19]

The earliest female mill operators were primarily the unmarried daughters of native Yankee farmers. Most of them worked in the mills only a few years before moving to marriage and occasionally school teaching. "Mill work was generally regarded as a desirable way to preserve young women from the moral perils of idleness," wrote Robert W. Smuts in his classic work *Women and Work in America* (1959). Between 1840 and 1860, Irish and French-Canadian immigrant women, many of them married, took over many of the mill jobs. Other immigrant women helped produce boots, shoes and cigars; toiled in printing plants and paper mills; or worked as housekeepers, chambermaids, charwomen, laundresses and cooks.

Civil War, Immigration and Labor Activity

The Civil War expanded the job opportunities for women, especially in office work, government service and retailing. Yet, in 1870, 70 per cent of the women who worked were still domestics. The average age of those employed was 23, and nearly 85 per cent were single and most contributed to the support of their families and lived with their parents. Their wages averaged $5.25 a week.

As immigrant women took over more of the industrial jobs, middle-class women began entering new occupations, such as teaching and social work. Mainly as a result of the Civil War, large numbers of women went into nursing and many stayed in the profession after the war. Despite these new opportunities, it was still rare for married women to work, especially in the middle classes, and even rarer for mothers to work. Among the four million working girls and women counted by the 1890 census, only half a million were married. A Bureau of Labor study of 17,000 women factory workers in 1887 found that only 4 per cent of them were married. Only one woman teacher out of 25 was married in 1890, partly because many communities would not hire married women. "Should a female teacher marry," declared the bylaws of New York City, "her place shall thereupon become vacant."[20]

By and large, married women worked only if their husbands

---

[19] Heidi I. Hartmann, "Women's Work in the United States" *Current History*, May 1976, p. 216.

[20] Cited in Robert W. Smuts' *Women and Work in America* (1959), p. 19.

were permanently or temporarily unable to support their families. Around the turn of the century, Smuts wrote, "When a married woman worked it was usually a sign that something had gone wrong." Only among blacks and the immigrant populations of New England textile towns was a large minority of wives employed outside the home. Among the blacks, according to the 1890 census, nearly one-fourth of the wives and nearly two-thirds of the widows were employed.

Partly because their options were so limited, many 19th century women eagerly embraced womanhood as a vocation in itself. The ideology of "True Womanhood," popularized through women's magazines such as *Godey's Lady's Book,* revolved around the notion that women's rightful place was in the home. However, this ideal was not readily attainable by most working-class women, who were more concerned with improving their working conditions.

Women industrial workers had formed local workingwomen's societies as early as the 1830s. "In the 1840s, women workers were in the leadership of labor militancy in the United States."[21] Women participated in attempts to form national unions in the 1860s and 1870s and in the Knights of Labor in the 1880s. At its height, the Knights of Labor had 50,000 women members—most of them organized into "separate but equal" locals. In 1886, the Knights hired the first woman investigator of female working conditions, Leonora Barry. But for the most part, women were discouraged from joining unions. "Keeping women out of the union was a way...to keep women out of the trade or to limit their participation."[22]

Nevertheless, women were active in the New England textile mill strikes conducted by the Industrial Workers of the World ("Wobblies") in 1912, and the AFL's International Ladies' Garment Workers Union began to organize vast numbers of women, many of them immigrants, in the needles trade in New York City in 1909. The tragic Triangle Fire in New York City in 1911, which killed 146 young women shirtmakers because the fire exits were locked, was a tremendous spur to organization. By 1920, the garment workers union had nearly 100,000 members.

Job Gains Coinciding With Push for Suffrage

World War I created new job opportunities for women, and thousands moved into jobs formerly held by men. Feminist leaders in the campaign for woman's suffrage were convinced that a new era of feminine equality was dawning. "Wonderful as

---

[21] Rosalynn Baxandall, Linda Gordon and Susan Reverby, eds., *America's Working Women* (1976), p. 66.
[22] *Ibid.*, pp. 83-84.

Women's Share of the U.S. Labor Force

1990*	43%	1955	31%
1976	41	1950	29
1970	38	1940	25
1965	35	1930	22
1960	33	1920	20

* Projected

Source: U.S. Department of Labor

this hour is for democracy and labor," Margaret Drier Robbins told the Women's Trade Union League in 1917, "it is the first hour in history for the women of the world.... At last, after centuries of disabilities and discrimination, women are coming into the labor and festival of life on equal terms with men."[23]

But it was not to be. After the war both employers and male employees assumed that women would happily relinquish the new jobs and skills that they had acquired. The male-dominated AFL unions led the fight for legislation to exclude women from such jobs they had held during the war as meter reading, streetcar conducting, taxi driving and elevator operating; they were also excluded from night work and overtime, which effectively eliminated them from fields like printing.

Despite these restrictions, more women were working than ever before. During the 1920s the female labor force grew to 10.7 million from 8.4 million, a 26 per cent increase. Single women of the middle classes were entering clerical and sales work in in-

---

[23] Quoted in William Henry Chafe, *The American Working Woman: Her Changing Social, Economic and Political Roles, 1920-1970* (1972), p. 49.

creasing numbers. "Even the girls who knew that they were going to be married pretended to be considering important business positions," Sinclair Lewis wrote in his 1920 novel, *Main Street*. Frederick Lewis Allen noted in *Only Yesterday* (1931), his account of the 1920s, that after passage of the suffrage amendment in 1919 middle-class girls "poured out of schools and colleges into all manner of occupations," But according to William Henry Chafe, historians have overstated the amount of economic change which occurred in the decade.

> There is no evidence that a revolution took place in women's economic role after World War I, nor can it be said that the 1920s represented a watershed in the history of women at work.... Aspiring career women were still limited to positions traditionally set aside for females; the overwhelming majority of American working women continued to toil at menial occupations for inadequate pay; and the drive to abolish economic discrimination enlisted little popular support.[24]

The number of married women entering the labor force steadily increased. By 1940, 17 per cent of all women who worked were married. Still many people continued to oppose married women working, particularly during the Depression. The Gallup Poll in 1936 found that 82 per cent of the population objected. In the late 1930s bills were introduced in 26 state legislatures to keep married women from holding jobs. Only one of these passed. This was in Louisiana, and it was later repealed.

Breakthrough in the World War II Job Market

World War II had profound effects on the U.S. economy, and particularly on women workers. As millions of men went into uniform, women went into industry as never before, accounting for 36 per cent of the nation's labor force in 1945, up from 25 per cent in 1940. Wages rose, the number of wives holding jobs doubled and unionization of women quadrupled. Employers' attitudes toward women remained skeptical, but since women were the only available labor, they were hired.

Black women found jobs in manufacturing for the first time. Previous bans on the employment of married women were discarded; by 1944, married women comprised almost half of the female labor force. The war gave women access to more skilled and higher-paying jobs. Although the war made rapid changes in women's economic status, it did not make a lasting or profound difference in the public attitude toward working women, nor did it lead to greater equality between the sexes. Women continued to receive less pay than men (65 per cent less in manufacturing), to be denied opportunities for training and advancement, and to work in separate job categories. During the

[24] Chafe, *op. cit*, p. 51.

war, concluded William Henry Chafe, "traditional attitudes toward women's place remained largely unchanged."[25]

After the war, women were expected to return to their traditional role of homemaker. Behind the efforts of employers, educators, social workers and the media to persuade women to leave the work force were two important economic considerations, said the editors of *America's Working Women:* "On the one hand, the system could not provide full employment; on the other hand, continued industrial profits required, with the diminution of military spending, an expansion in the consumption of household durable goods. An emphasis on 'homemaking' encouraged women to buy."[26]

This view overlooked the fact that the majority of women were working for economic reasons. A Department of Labor survey in 1945 found that 96 per cent of all single women, 98 per cent of the widowed and divorced women, and 57 per cent of the married women seriously needed to continue working after the war. Many women were laid off in the heavy industries. But for the most part, these women did not return to their kitchens. Instead, they found work in the traditional areas still available to them. These were the only options open to many women until the 1960s, when anti-discrimination legislation opened up new opportunities.

Laws Banning Discrimination in Employment

Laws dealing with sex discrimination in employment have been enacted on both the federal and state levels in the past 15 years, beginning with the federal Equal Pay Act of 1963. It required all employers subject to the Fair Labor Standards Act[27] to provide equal pay for men and women performing similar work. In 1972, coverage of this act was extended to executives, administrators and professionals, including all employees of private and public educational institutions.

The courts have held that jobs do not have to be identical, only "substantially equal," for the Equal Pay Act to apply. In a well-publicized case involving the Corning Glass Works, the Supreme Court ruled in 1974 that shift differences (with men working at night and women working during the day) did not make the working conditions of the men and women dissimilar and thus would not justify a higher wage for the men.[28]

---

[25] Chafe, *op. cit.,* p. 188. See also Lyn Goldfarb, "Separated & Unequal: Discrimination Against Women Workers After World War II (The U.A.W. 1944-54)," The Women's Work Project, 1976.

[26] Rosalyn Baxandall, et al., *op. cit.,* pp. 282-283.

[27] The Fair Labor Standards Act of 1938 established a minimum wage for individuals engaged in interstate commerce or the production of goods for commerce. The law has been amended from time to time to increase the minimum rate and to extend coverage to new groups of employees.

[28] *Corning Glass Works v. Brennan,* 417 U.S. 188 (1974).

A milestone in equal employment opportunity for women was reached with the passage of the Civil Rights Act of 1964. Title VII of that act prohibited discrimination based on sex—as well as race, religion and national origin—in hiring or firing, wages and salaries, promotions or any terms, conditions or privileges of employment. Exceptions were permitted only when sex was a bona fide occupational qualification, as in the case of an actor or a wet nurse. Title VII is administered by the Equal Employment Opportunity Commission, whose five members are appointed by the President. Initially, the powers of the EEOC were limited largely to investigation and conciliation, but Congress amended the act in 1972 to let the agency go directly to court to enforce the law. The 1972 amendments also provided that discrimination charges could be filed by organizations on behalf of aggrieved individuals, as well as by employees and job applicants themselves.

Because sex discrimination sometimes took forms different from race discrimination, the EEOC issued sex-discrimination guidelines. They stated that the refusal to hire an individual cannot be based on assumed employment characteristics of women in general, and that the preferences of customers or existing employees should not be the basis for refusing to hire an individual. The guidelines also prohibited hiring based on classification or labeling of "men's jobs" and "women's jobs," or advertising under male and female headings.

The EEOC guidelines declared that state laws that prohibited or limited the employment of women—in certain occupations, in jobs requiring the lifting or carrying of specified weights, for more than a specified number of hours, during certain hours of the night, and immediately before and after child-birth—discriminate on the basis of sex because they do not take into account individual capacities and preferences. A series of court cases upheld this guideline, and according to the Bureau of Labor's "1975 Handbook on Women Workers," the conflict between state and federal laws on this point "was for the most part resolved in the early 1970s." In a case involving the guidelines, the Supreme Court ruled in 1971[29] that discrimination need not be intentional to be unlawful.

In October 1967, President Johnson issued an executive order barring sex discrimination and other forms of bias in hiring by federal contractors. Executive Order 11246 required federal contractors to take "affirmative action to ensure that applicants are employed and that they are treated during employment without regard to their race, color, religion, sex or national origin."[30]

---

[29] *Griggs et al. v. Duke Power Co.*, 401 U.S. 424 (1971).
[30] See "Reverse Discrimination," *E.R.R.*, 1976, Vol. II, pp. 561-580. See also *Affirmative Action For Women* (1975), by Dorothy Jongeward and Dru Scott.

Working Wives

The age of the two paycheck family has arrived. Since 1960, the number of families in which both husband and wife work has jumped to 42 per cent from 29 per cent. In 1976 alone an additional one million wives joined their husbands in the work force, according to the Department of Labor. The prime reason for their working was to help keep up with family bills.

During the 1950s the largest increase in labor force participation was among married women beyond the usual childbearing years (20 to 34). In recent years, however, there has been a sharp upturn in labor force participation of young married women, especially among married women with small children. Of the 21.1 million wives in the work force in March 1975, over half—11.4 million—had children under 18 years of age.

Why the dramatic upturn in working mothers? Perhaps one reason is that economists now estimate that it costs between $70,-000 and $100,000 to raise a child for the first 18 years of his or her life.*

*Reported by the Association of American Colleges in "Project on the Status and Education of Women," October 1976.

Other federal laws, orders and regulations have prohibited employment discrimination in special occupations or industries. For example, Title IX of the Education Amendments of 1972[31] specifically prohibited sex discrimination in education. Other laws and rules required affirmative action for minorities and women in construction and maintenance of the Alaska Pipeline.

The campaign to wipe out sex discrimination has resulted in court decisions and out-of-court settlements costing employers hundreds of millions of dollars in back pay and other benefits. Perhaps the most significant settlements were the two that the EEOC arranged with American Telephone & Telegraph Co. The first, signed January 1973, applied mostly to women and also to minority-group males who had been denied equal pay and promotion opportunities in non-management jobs. The agency ordered AT&T to award them $15-million in back pay and up to $23-million in pay increases. The second settlement, filed in May 1974, provided similar awards to management employees who were victims of illegal sex discrimination in pay. "The AT&T decision was important for symbolic reasons...," said Isabel Sawhill, a labor-market economist at the Urban Institute in Washington. "It established that companies have to look at their patterns of employment."[32]

[31] Amendments to the Higher Education Act of 1965, the Vocational Education Act of 1963, the General Education Provisions Act, and the Elementary and Secondary Education Act of 1965.

[32] Quoted in *Newsweek*, Dec. 16, 1976, p. 69. Other big cases subsequently have involved the Bank of America and the brokerage firm of Merrill Lynch.

Continuing Fight for Job Equality

DESPITE THESE VICTORIES, there still is widespread discrimination against women in the workplace. Many feminists say the problem lies not with the anti-discrimination laws and regulations, but with the enforcement efforts of the Equal Employment Opportunity Commission. The General Accounting Office, an investigative arm of Congress, reported recently: "Although the EEOC has had some success in obtaining relief for victims of discrimination in specific instances, it does not appear to have yet made the substantial advances against employment discrimination which will be necessary to make a real difference in the employment status of minorities and women."[33]

The backlog of discrimination complaints has risen to nearly 130,000, according to *The Washington Post*, Feb. 6, 1977. Workers who file complaints frequently wait years even to be told whether their charges have merit. By then, the worker may have given up and found other employment. The General Accounting Office said that nearly half (47.7 per cent) of the cases completed by the EEOC between July 1, 1972, and March 31, 1975, were "administrative closures," meaning that the worker could no longer be found or had lost interest in pursuing the charge. Only 11 per cent of the cases resolved during that period involved successfully negotiated settlements. According to the General Accounting Office, an individual has only one chance in 33 of having the charge settled successfully in the year it is filed. The average case takes nearly two years to settle.

In its 11-year history, the agency has had six successive chairmen and 10 executive directors. Not one chairman has completed his full five-year term. The position has been vacant since May 1976, when Lowell W. Perry resigned after one year in office. The agency's acting director, Ethel Bent Walsh, an EEOC commissioner since 1971, counts it as a sign of progress that the commissioners now meet and discuss problems. "When I first came here we didn't even talk to each other unless we met in the hall," she told the *Post*.

Dissension among the five commissioners may be inherent in the structure of the commission, according to Eleanor Holmes Norton, head of the New York City Commission on Equal Opportunity. "A commission structure involving five highly paid

---

[33] "The Equal Employment Opportunity Commission Has Made Limited Progress in Eliminating Employment Discrimination," Report to the Congress by the Comptroller General of the United States, Sept. 28, 1976.

presidential appointees, as EEOC now has, assumes that *policy* as opposed to *operational questions* will predominate," she said recently. "Administering an already unwieldy ship with what at times are five captains must be especially difficult in a period when operational problems are out of hand."[34] Her suggestion for improving EEOC operations—abolish the commission and appoint a single boss.

Other criticism has been directed toward the EEOC staff. In a recent article in *Fortune* magazine, Dorothy Rabinowitz accused the agency of being biased toward blacks at the expense of women and other minorities.[35] One reason for the agency's possible bias in favor of blacks, said Robert Ellis Smith, a former civil rights executive at the Department of Health, Education and Welfare, is that many of the senior positions are filled with alumni of the southern civil rights battles.[36] Acting Director Walsh told a House subcommittee in 1975 that many of the complaint investigators were "not of the caliber we required and have insufficient training." The National Commission on the Observance of International Women's Year in 1976 recommended that the EEOC "make a substantial effort to upgrade the quality of training of its personnel.[37]

Attempt to Nullify Court Ruling on Pregnancy Pay

Women's rights groups and organized labor plan to lobby this year for legislation to ensure sick pay for working women on leave because of pregnancy and thus counteract a recent Supreme Court ruling. The court held, on Dec. 7, 1976, that General Electric could exclude pregnancy from its employee disability insurance benefits without violating the 1964 Civil Rights Act. Writing for the court's 6-3 majority, Justice William H. Rehnquist said the exclusion was not discriminatory because "there is no risk from which men are protected and women are not...." In dissent, Justice William J. Brennan Jr.[38] wrote: "Surely it offends common sense to suggest...that a classification revolving around pregnancy is not, at the minimum, strongly 'sex related.' "

The business community generally applauded the decision. It saved American business $1.6-billion, the American Society for Personnel Administration estimated. In contrast, Karen

[34] Quoted by Robert Ellis Smith in "The EEOC and How to Make it Work," *Ms.* February 1977, p. 64. See also "A Look at What is Happening in Fight on Job Discrimination," *U.S. News & World Report*, Dec. 13, 1976, pp. 35-36.

[35] Dorothy Rabinowitz, "The Bias in the Government's Anti-Bias Agency," *Fortune*, December 1976, p. 138.

[36] Smith, *op. cit.*, p. 103.

[37] "To Form a More Perfect Union: Justice for American Women," Report of the National Commission on the Observance of International Women's Year, June 1976, p. 192. Walsh made her comments before the House Appropriations Subcommittee on State, Justice, Commerce, the Judiciary and Related Agencies on May 6, 1975.

[38] Also dissenting were Justices Thurgood Marshall and John Paul Stevens in the case, *General Electric v. Gilbert*, 429 U.S. 1976.

DeCrow, president of the National Organization for Women, called the ruling a "slap in the face to motherhood," and added, "If people are paid sick leave when they're out for nose jobs, hair transplants and vasectomies, why not for childbirth?"[39] In addition to lobbying for legislative remedies, union representatives plan to push for collective bargaining agreements with large employers that would ensure disability pay for women during pregnancy. It is estimated that 40 per cent of all U.S. companies have disability plans, and approximately 40 per cent of those include some maternity benefits.

Most criticism of the EEOC has focused on the backlog of cases. Initially it was thought that no more than 2,000 complaints a year would be filed, but in fiscal 1976 alone 75,173 were filed. Contributing to the agency's inability to cope with the growing number of complaints was a policy change in 1968. That year the agency began shifting much of its staff away from processing individual complaints in order to undertake broad investigations into widespread discriminatory patterns of certain corporations and industries. Some say the EEOC should abandon the case-by-case approach altogether. But many feminists oppose this idea. "The whole purpose of Title VII," said Judith Lichtman of the Women's Legal Defense Fund, "was to remove the burden from individual employees and make the government investigate complaints." Perry, the former commissioner, wonders whether the EEOC ought not to be abolished entirely and its responsibilities turned over to the Justice Department. But the agency's supporters credit it with fostering an atmosphere that encourages job equity.

Psychic Barriers to Women's Advancement

In many instances the barriers to women are not overt discrimination. Psychologists say working women are frequently handicapped by a weak self-image and lack of confidence. In a classic study in 1968, psychologist Matina Horner, now president of Radcliffe College, concluded that as a result of their childhood training and various social pressures of home and family, many women are hobbled by a "fear of success"—an acquired fear that the risks of succeeding are "loss of femininity."

The reasons for the absence of women in top management positions go beyond the "fear of success" syndrome, according to Margaret Hennig and Anne Jardim, co-directors of the Simmons College graduate program in management. They found that women's attitudes toward work are totally different from men's and that this impedes women's progress in the male-dominated corporate world. Men, they said, tend to have long-term career goals, while women are likelier to focus on short-

---

[39] Quoted in *The New York Times*, Dec. 16, 1976.

The Secretary Trap

An experiment conducted recently at the University of Maryland demonstrated the tendency of employers to shunt women into secretarial jobs. Male and female students, all white so that racial bias would not enter the picture, and all equally qualified, applied for jobs at 39 employment agencies.

Seventy-seven per cent of the men and 59 per cent of the women received job offers. Among the men, nine of ten job offers were for administrative or managerial positions and the rest were clerical. For the women, 82 per cent were clerical and 17 per cent were managerial. All of the women applicants were asked to take typing tests. The men were interviewed about their interests, ambitions and favorite sports.

term planning, largely because they have been brought up to think of careers conditionally—as an alternative to marriage. This ambiguity causes women to make their career decisions late, about the age of 30 to 33, while men generally build the foundations of their careers while they are still in their twenties.

Women are further hindered, according to Hennig and Jardim, by their lack of exposure to the informal factors that govern a man's world—contacts built up through clubs and golf games, or "old boy" relationships often started in college. "In the competition for career advancement...men have a clear advantage over women."[40] To help women overcome some of these disadvantages, some employers are encouraging their female employees to attend assertiveness training courses and other programs designed to enhance their self-image.

Changing women's attitudes may take some time. But there are other factors hindering women's participation in the labor force. One-third of the working women have children to care for. There are 6.5 million children under the age of 6, and 18 million others 6 to 14, whose mothers work. Yet according to the latest government estimates, care in licensed day-care centers is available for only slightly more than one million children.[41]

The burdens of child care for working mothers are compounded by other household responsibilities. Although men are doing more of the child rearing and housework these days, the women still bear the brunt of it. Despite all the difficulties, working women show no signs of abandoning their new roles in the work force. However, more and more working women are demanding that society and their families adjust to the new realities of women's lives.

---

[40] Margaret Hennig and Anne Jardim, "Women Executives in the Old-Boy Network," *Psychology Today*, January 1977, p. 81.
[41] See "Child Care," *E.R.R.*, 1972 Vol. I, pp. 441-460, and "Single-Parent Families," *E.R.R.*, 1976 Vol. II, pp. 661-680.

Selected Bibliography

Books

Baxandall, Rosalyn, Linda Gordon and Susan Reverby, *America's Working Women*, Vintage Books, 1976.

Bird, Caroline, *Born Female: The High Cost of Keeping Women Down*, Pocket Books, 1971.

——*Enterprising Women*, New American Library, 1976.

Chafe, William Henry, *The American Woman: Her Changing Social, Economic and Political Roles, 1920-1970*, Oxford University Press, 1972.

Jongeward, Dorothy and Dru Scott, *Affirmative Action for Women*, Addison-Wesley, 1975.

Kreps, Juanita, *Sex in the Marketplace: American Women at Work*, The Johns Hopkins Press, 1971.

Smuts, Robert W., *Women and Work in America*, Schocken, 1959.

Articles

"A Powerful New Role in the Work Force," *U.S. News & World Report*, Dec. 8, 1975.

Cowley, Susan Cheever, "Women at Work," *Newsweek*, Dec. 6, 1976.

Hartmann, Heidi I., "Women's Work in the United States," *Current History*, May 1976.

Hennig, Margaret and Anne Jardim, "Women Executives in the Old-Boy Network," *Psychology Today*, January 1977.

Kron, Joan, "The Dual Career Dilemma," *New York*, Oct. 25, 1976.

Rabinowitz, Dorothy, "The Bias in the Government's Anti-Bias Agency," *Fortune*, December 1976.

Smith, Robert Ellis, "The Equal Employment Opportunity Commission and How to Make It Work," *Ms*, February 1977.

"Women of the Year: Great Changes, New Chances, Tough Choices," *Time*, Jan. 5, 1976.

Reports and Studies

Editorial Research Reports, "Child Care," 1972 Vol. II, p. 439; "Single-Parent Families," 1976 Vol. II, p. 661; "Status of Women," 1970 Vol. II, p. 565.

Goldfarb, Lyn, "Separated and Unequal: Discrimination Against Women Workers After World War II (The U.A.W. 1944-1954)," The Women's Work Project, 1976.

Morrison, Peter A. and Judith P. Wheeler, "Working Women and 'Woman's Work': A Demographic Perspective on the Breakdown of Sex Roles," The Rand Corporation, June 1976.

"The Equal Employment Opportunity Commission Has Made Limited Progress in Eliminating Employment Discrimination," General Accounting Office, Sept. 28, 1976.

U.S. Department of Labor, "The Earnings Gap Between Women and Men," October 1976.

—— "U.S. Working Women: A Chartbook," 1975.

—— "Why Women Work," July 1976.

—— "Women Workers Today," October 1976.

—— "1975 Handbook on Women Workers," 1975.

Reverse Discrimination

by

Sandra Stencel

Aug. 6
1 9 7 6

REVERSE DISCRIMINATION

I N TEXAS, two white employees of a Houston trucking firm were fired in 1970 after being charged with stealing 60 one-gallon cans of antifreeze from a customer's shipment. A black worker charged with the same offense was kept on.

In Virginia, 328 men and 57 women applied for two full-time positions in the sociology and anthropology department of Virginia Commonwealth University. No men were interviewed for the jobs; two women were hired.

In Chicago, on Jan. 5, 1976, U.S. District Court Judge Prentice H. Marshall gave the city 90 days to hire 400 new police officers. Of these, 200 were to be black and Spanish-named men and 66 were to be women. The judge also imposed a similar quota on future hiring.

In California, a white student was denied admission to the law school at the University of California's Davis campus in 1975 even though he had better grades and test scores than 74 other applicants admitted under a special minority admissions program.

These incidents and others like them have sparked an increasingly bitter debate over what has come to be known as "reverse discrimination"—giving preferential treatment to women, blacks and persons from other minority groups in such areas as employment and college admissions. The policy is defended as fair and necessary to compensate for past discrimination. It is criticized as "robbing Peter to pay Paul." The critics say that all persons should be judged solely on their personal qualifications.

The furor stems from the government's decade-old policy of requiring educators and employers to take "affirmative action" to prevent racial or sexual discrimination. To make up for alleged past discriminatory hiring practices, the government forced businesses and organizations holding federal contracts to set up goals and timetables for hiring minorities and women. Many employers complain that they are trapped between the government's demands to increase opportunities for women and minorities on the one hand, and, on the other, charges by white males that affirmative action constitutes reverse discrimination.

Growing numbers of white males, charging that they are victims of reverse discrimination, are going to court seeking redress. "The suits present a thorny problem for the courts," said *U.S. News & World Report.* "On the one hand, the preferences being attacked have a legally sanctioned goal—the correction or prevention of racial or sexual bias. But those not covered by such preferences charge it is just as illegal to discriminate against whites and males as against minorities and women."[1]

A recent ruling by the U.S. Supreme Court could result in a significant increase in lawsuits charging reverse discrimination. The Court ruled on June 25, 1976, that the Civil Rights Acts of 1866 and 1964 protect white people as well as blacks against racial discrimination. The ruling was the result of a suit filed by the two white employees of the Houston trucking firm who were fired for stealing company cargo although a black man who participated in the theft was not. With the help of the U.S. Equal Employment Opportunity Commission, the two men sued the company and their union on discrimination charges. The case was dismissed in lower federal court, which held that only minority group members could bring such charges under these laws. But on appeal the Supreme Court ruled the suit valid and held that the two civil rights laws ban discrimination against whites "upon the same standards as would be applicable were they Negroes."

The full meaning of the court's decision is not yet clear. To some observers it appeared to cast doubt on hiring and promotion quotas that favor blacks and women over white males. However, Justice Thurgood Marshall, author of the majority opinion, said the Court was not considering the legality of affirmative action programs.

Suits by White Males Charging Discrimination

The Supreme Court earlier had sidestepped a decision on reverse discrimination in the highly publicized DeFunis case *(see p. 54).* The plaintiff, Marco DeFunis, charged that he had been turned down by the University of Washington Law School while minority applicants with lower grades and test scores were admitted. When the Court in 1974 refused to decide the case on its merits, four justices dissented. One of the four, William J. Brennan, said: "Few constitutional questions in recent years have stirred as much debate, and they will not disappear. They must inevitably return to the federal courts and ultimately again to this court."

Several cases alleging reverse discrimination are expected to come before the Supreme Court in the near future. A definitive

---

[1] " 'Reverse Discrimination'—Has It Gone Too Far?" *U.S. News & World Report,* March 29, 1976, p. 26.

AT&T Cases

The legal complexities involved in reverse discrimination are perhaps best illustrated by a recent court ruling against American Telephone and Telegraph Co. In 1973, after more than two years of litigation, AT&T agreed to hire and promote thousands of women and minority group members. Following the guidelines laid out in their court-approved affirmative action plan, AT&T promoted a woman service representative over a male employee who had more experience and seniority. The man sued, contending that he was a victim of sex discrimination.

On June 9, 1976, U.S. District Court Judge Gerhard Gesell of Washington, D.C., ordered AT&T to pay the man an undetermined sum in damages. Although Judge Gesell held that the company had acted correctly in promoting the woman, he went on to say that the impact of its past discriminatory policies should fall on the company, not on "an innocent employee who had earned promotion." On the other hand, Gesell ruled that the man was entitled only to damages. To award him the promotion he was denied "might well perpetuate and prolong the effects of the discrimination [the 1973 agreement] was designed to eliminate."

If Judge Gesell's opinion is upheld by the higher courts, employers will face yet another expensive cost in complying with court orders to correct past discriminatory employment practices.

---

ruling would provide welcome guidance to the lower courts which have handed down contradictory rulings. In several recent cases the courts have ruled in favor of men who charged that employers were giving preferential treatment to women and minorities. For example, on June 9, U.S. District Court Judge Gerhard Gesell of Washington, D.C., ordered the American Telephone & Telegraph Co. to pay damages to a male employee passed over for promotion in favor of a less-experienced woman *(see box above)*.

Another federal judge in the District of Columbia, Oliver Gasch, ruled on July 28 that Georgetown University's policy of setting aside 60 per cent of its first-year law school scholarships for minority students constituted reverse discrimination and therefore violated the 1964 Civil Rights Act. The ruling came in a suit filed by a white student, J. Michael Flanagan, who claimed he was discriminated against because no more scholarships were available for white students by the time he had been admitted to the law school, although scholarship funds still were available for minority students.

In the case involving Virginia Commonwealth University, U.S. District Court Judge D. Dortch Warriner of Richmond ruled on May 28 that the school had acted illegally when it gave hiring preferences to women over equally qualified male applicants. The suit was filed by Dr. James Albert Cramer, a professor with

47

temporary status in the school's sociology department and one of the 328 men to apply for full-time positions. Cramer contended that the university, in denying him a job because he was male, violated the Fourteenth Amendment's guarantee of equal protection under the law and the Civil Rights Act which bans discrimination on the basis of race, color, religion, sex or national origin. The university argued that under state and federal guidelines it was required to take affirmative action to hire women and minorities to "eliminate the effects of past discrimination" against them.

Judge Warriner held that under the equal-protection clause, "where sex is the sole factor upon which differential treatment is determined, there is no constitutional justification for treating the sexes differently." He said that even if the university was guilty of past discrimination, its preferential policies were unconstitutional because the civil rights law prohibits employment practices that "predicate hiring and promotion decisions on gender-based criteria."

In contrast, some other recent court rulings have upheld preferential treatment as a legal way of overcoming the effects of past discrimination. For example, the New York State Court of Appeals on April 8 held that the Brooklyn Downstate Medical Center had acted properly when it gave certain admissions preferences to minority applicants. The court said that reverse discrimination was constitutional "in proper circumstances." The test of constitutionality, the court held, should be "whether preferential treatment satisfies a substantial state interest.... It need be found that, on balance, the gain to be derived from the preferential policy outweighs its possible detrimental effects."

Case For and Against Preferential Treatment

Many of those who advocate preferential hiring and admissions policies deny that it amounts to reverse discrimination. "There is no such thing as reverse discrimination," said Herbert Hill, national labor director for the National Association for the Advancement of Colored People. "Those who complain of it are engaging in a deliberate attempt to perpetuate the racial status quo by drawing attention away from racial discrimination to make the remedy the issue. The real issue remains racial discrimination."[2]

Others, while acknowledging the dilemmas posed by preferential treatment, insist that such policies are necessary to wipe out the effects of past discrimination. "While there may be an element of unfairness in preferential treatment," said the authors of a law journal article, "some price must be paid to overcome

---

[2] Quoted in " 'Reverse Discrimination'—Has It Gone Too Far?" *U.S. News & World Report,* March 29, 1976, p. 29.

Preferential Treatment: Two Views

"Preferential remedies to end employment discrimination may be likened to starting one controlled forest fire in order to bring a raging one under control. At first the idea may seem illogical, but the remedial principle is sound."

—Professors Harry T. Edwards
and Barry L. Zaretsky
Michigan Law Review

"There is no constitutional right for any race to be preferred."

—Supreme Court Justice
William O. Douglas in
DeFunis v. Odegaard

"...[A] preference which aids minorities is perfectly consistent with the purpose of the Fourteenth Amendment."

—Brief submitted to Supreme Court
in *De Funis v. Odegaard*

"Where individuals have overcome individual hardship, they should be favored, but what offends me deeply is the shorthand we use, which is race."

—Professor Alan Dershowitz of
Harvard Law School quoted
in *The New Republic*

"The reverse discrimination aspect of affirmative action is, in reality, the removal of that benefit which American society has so long bestowed, without question, upon its privileged classes."

—Shirley E. Stewart,
Cleveland State Law Review

the longstanding pervasive patterns of race and sex bias in this nation. The minor injustice that may result...is, on balance, outweighed by the fact that temporary preferential remedies appear to be the only way to effectively break the cycle of employment discrimination and open all levels of the job market to all qualified applicants."[3]

Affirmative action, it is pointed out, is not the first government program to prescribe differential treatment as a social policy. The Veterans Preference Act of 1944 stipulated that veterans should be given special consideration when seeking employment with the federal government. This statute granted persons extra points on competitive civil service examinations solely because they were veterans.

Economic statistics also provide an argument for the preferential treatment of minorities and women. According to the Census Bureau's latest findings, for 1974, black families had a median income of $7,808—half of the families earned more and half earned less. That was only 58 per cent of the white families' median income ($13,356), a drop of three percentage points since 1969.[4] There is a similar—and widening—gap between the earnings of men and women. The Department of Labor reported the median income of full-time women workers in 1975 was $6,975 while that of men was $12,152; women's earnings thus were only 57 per cent as high as men's, down from 64 per cent in 1955. *The Wall Street Journal* observed: "The average female college graduate earned less last year than the average male high-school dropout."[5]

Critics of affirmative action charge that the original purpose of that policy—the achievement of full and equal employment and educational opportunities—has been perverted. This theme dominates a controversial new book, *Affirmative Discrimination: Ethnic Inequality and Public Policy* (1975) by Harvard sociologist Nathan Glazer. He wrote: "In the early 1970s, affirmative action came to mean much more than advertising opportunities actively, seeking out those who might not know of them, and preparing those who might not yet be qualified. It came to mean the setting of statistical requirements based on race, color and national origin...." As a consequence of this shift in policy, Glazer said, "Those groups that are not considered eligible for special benefits become resentful."

---

[3] Harry T. Edwards and Barry L. Zaretsky, "Preferential Remedies for Employment Discrimination," *Michigan Law Review*, November 1975, p. 7. Edwards is a professor of law at the University of Michigan and Zaretsky is an assistant professor of law at Wayne State University.

[4] See U.S. Bureau of the Census, Current Population Reports, Special Studies, Series P-23 No. 54, "The Social and Economic Status of Black Population in the United States, 1974."

[5] *The Wall Street Journal*, July 6, 1976. See also U.S. Department of Labor, "1975 Handbook on Women Workers," and Lester C. Thurow's "The Economic Status of Minorities and Women," *Civil Rights Digest*, winter-spring 1976, pp. 3-9.

Glazer also raised the question of which groups should qualify for special treatment.

> The statistical basis for redress makes one great error: All "whites" are consigned to the same category, deserving of no special consideration. That is not the way "whites" see themselves, or indeed are, in social reality. Some may be "whites," pure and simple. But almost all have some specific ethnic or religious identification, which, to the individual involved, may mean a distinctive history of past—or perhaps some present—discrimination.

"Compensation for the past is a dangerous principle," Glazer went on to say. "It can be extended indefinitely and make for endless trouble."

Disputes Over Hiring and Admissions in Academia

The backlash against affirmative action and preferential treatment has been particularly strong in the academic community. "By using statistics to determine the presence of discrimination and ignoring differences in qualifications, the federal government is undermining the integrity and scholarly function of the university," Professor Allan C. Ornstein of Loyola University of Chicago has written.[6] Government intrusion into more and more aspects of university life was the theme of the 1974-1975 annual report issued recently by Harvard President Derek Bok.

> In a few short years [he said], universities have been encumbered with a formidable body of regulations, some of which seem unnecessary and most of which cause needless confusion, administrative expense and red tape. If this process continues, higher education will almost certainly lose some of the independence, the flexibility and the diversity that have helped it to flourish in the past.

Bok was particularly concerned about the mounting costs of complying with federal regulations.[7] It has been reported elsewhere, for example, that when Reed College in Portland, Ore., sought to hire some new faculty members recently, it was told by the Department of Health, Education and Welfare—which is responsible for administering affirmative action programs in educational institutions—to advertise nationally instead of going through normal academic channels. As a result, the small private college was flooded with some 6,000 applications. In addition, HEW demanded that Reed keep records on all the applicants not hired and make detailed reports on prime candidates who reached the finals, including their race, sex, qualifications, prior experience, and why Reed did not hire

---

[6] Allan C. Ornstein, "Quality, Not Quotas," *Society*, January-February 1976, p. 10.
[7] See "Future of Private Colleges," *E.R.R.*, 1976 Vol. I, pp. 305-322.

them.[8] The University of California at Berkeley has estimated that it will spend some $400,000 to implement an affirmative action plan.

Some educators charge that the government is forcing colleges to hire underqualified and unqualified persons merely because they are women or members of a minority group. Colleges that fail to comply face the loss of federal funds which can amount to millions of dollars. In 1971, for example, HEW froze $13-million in federal research contracts with Columbia University when the school failed to come up with an acceptable affirmative action plan. Educators often tell the story of the HEW representative who, when informed that there were no black teachers in the religion department of Brown University because none who applied met the requirements for ancient languages, replied: "Then end these old-fashioned programs that require irrelevant languages."[9]

HEW has shown some sensitivity to the special characteristics of academic employment. In December 1974 it reviewed the existing codes applying to affirmative action. This "memorandum to college and university presidents," signed by Peter E. Holmes, director of the department's Office of Civil Rights, stated that under existing law, colleges and universities could hire the "best qualified" person for a position. The memo concluded that the legal commitment to affirmative action merely required a school to show "good faith attempts" to recruit women and minorities.

What disturbs some eduators more than reverse discrimination are signs that preferential admissions to professional schools have brought in students who cannot do the work. Dr. Bernard D. Davis, a professor of bacterial physiology at Harvard Medical School, suggested recently that academic standards in the nation's medical schools have fallen in recent years because of the rise in the number of students with "substandard academic qualifications."

"It would be a rare person today," he wrote in *The New England Journal of Medicine*, "who would question the value of stretching the criteria for admission, and of trying to make up for earlier educational disadvantages...." But in their eagerness to help disadvantaged students, he charged, some medical schools are graduating students who may not be qualified to be doctors. He cited the example of one unidentified student who had been awarded a degree although he failed to pass a mandatory examination in five attempts. "It would be cruel," Dr. Davis wrote, "to admit students who have a very low probability of measuring up to reasonable standards. It is even crueler to abandon those

---

[8] See Ralph Kinney Bennett's "Colleges Under the Federal Gun," *Readers Digest,* May 1976, p. 126.
[9] The university later received an apology from HEW for the representative's remarks.

standards and allow the trusting patients to pay for our irresponsibility."[10]

The number of black students in American medical schools has increased greatly in recent years, from 783 in 1968 to 3,456 in 1976, in part because of special-admission efforts. There is also evidence of a higher failure rate among black students. At the University of Michigan Medical School, for example, the failure rate is 20 per cent for blacks and 4 per cent for whites. Recent medical school graduates of predominantly black Howard University, *The Washington Post* has reported, have failed their national board examinations—the final tests most medical school graduates take to become doctors—at a rate three and a half times above the national average.

Those who support preferential admissions to medical schools say that grades and test scores are not always a good indication of who will make good doctors. Said Dr. Alvin Poussaint, dean of student affairs at Harvard Medical School, "We need caring doctors, doctors with concerns and abilities not disclosed on the standards tests."[11]

Development of Affirmative Action

WHEN CONGRESS passed the Civil Rights Act in 1964, it was generally believed that discrimination took place primarily through conscious, overt actions against individuals. But it quickly became apparent that the processes of discrimination were much more subtle and complex than originally envisioned. It was discovered that normal, seemingly neutral policies such as seniority, aptitude and personnel tests, high school diploma requirements and college admission tests could perpetuate the effects of past discrimination. This led to the development of the affirmative action concept.

The need for affirmative action was spelled out by President Johnson in a commencement address at Howard University on June 4, 1965.

> Freedom is not enough [Johnson said]. You do not wipe out scars of centuries by saying "now you're free to go where you want and do as you desire." You do not take a person who for years has been hobbled by chains and liberate him, bringing him up to the

---

[10] Bernard D. Davis, "Academic Standards in Medical Schools," *The New England Journal of Medicine*, May 13, 1976. His article drew widespread criticism, including charges of racism, and he subsequently said it had been misrepresented in the press.

[11] Quoted in *The Washington Post*, June 1, 1976.

starting line of a race and then say "you're free to compete" and justly believe that you have been completely fair.

The following Sept. 24 Johnson issued Executive Order 11246 requiring federal contractors "to take affirmative action to ensure that applicants are employed, and that employees are treated during employment, without regard to their race, creed, color or national origin."[12] Every major contractor—one having more than 50 employees and a contract of $50,000 or more with the federal government—was required to submit a "written affirmative action compliance program" which would be monitored by the Department of Labor's Office of Federal Contract Compliance.

In January 1970, Secretary of Labor George P. Schulz issued guidelines for the affirmative action plans required by the executive order. The guidelines, which were revised in December 1971, stated that affirmative action was "results oriented." A contractor who was considered to have too few women or minority employees had to establish goals for each job classification, by sex and race, and timetables specifying the date when the situation would be corrected.

Philadelphia Plan Controversy Over Job Quotas

The Department of Labor had already—on June 29, 1969—announced a plan to increase minority employment in the construction trades in Philadelphia. The "Philadelphia Plan" set goals for the number of blacks and other minority workers to be hired on construction projects financed by federal funds. Secretary Schulz stressed that contractors who could not meet the hiring goals would not be penalized if they showed a "good faith effort" to fulfill them.

Controversy over the plan arose on Aug. 5 when Comptroller General Elmer B. Staats[13] issued a ruling that the Philadelphia Plan violated the 1964 Civil Rights Act by requiring racial hiring quotas. Staats dismissed the plan's distinction between a quota system and a goal system as "largely a matter of semantics." The purpose of either, he said, was to have contractors commit themselves to considering race or national origin in hiring new employees.

The Nixon administration continued to defend the plan. It pointed out that Congress had given the Attorney General, not the Comptroller General, authority to interpret the 1964 Civil Rights Act and that Attorney General John Mitchell had approved the Philadelphia Plan. It was incorrect, Mitchell said in a statement issued Sept. 22, 1969, to say that the 1964 act forbade

---

[12] Executive Order 11246 was amended in 1967 to apply to sexual discrimination.
[13] The Comptroller General of the United States works for Congress, not the executive branch.

employers to make race a factor in hiring employees. "The legal definition of discrimination is an evolving one," he said, "but it is now well recognized in judicial opinions that the obligation of non-discrimination, whether imposed by statute or by the Constitution, does not require, and, in some circumstances, may not permit obliviousness or indifference to the racial consequences of alternative courses of action...."

The Department of Labor put the Philadelphia Plan into effect the next day and soon afterward announced that similar plans would become effective in New York, Seattle, Boston, Los Angeles, San Francisco, St. Louis, Detroit, Pittsburgh and Chicago. The AFL-CIO and the building trades unions actively opposed such plans and lobbied for the inclusion of a provision in a 1970 appropriations bill to give the Comptroller General authority to block funds for any federal programs he considered to be illegal. Congress narrowly defeated this provision after President Nixon threatened to veto the appropriations bill if it was included. Critics of the Philadelphia Plan then turned to the courts, but in 1971 the plan was upheld in federal appeals court.[14]

Extension of Rules to Education; DeFunis Case

Educational institutions originally were not covered by the fair-employment section of the 1964 Civil Rights Act. This oversight was amended by the Equal Employment Act of 1972. "Discrimination against minorities and women in the field of education is as pervasive as discrimination in any other area of employment," said the House Committee on Education and Labor at the time. Similar views were expressed by the Senate Committee on Labor and Public Welfare: "As in other areas of employment, statistics for educational institutions indicate that minorities and women are precluded from the most prestigious and higher-paying positions, and are relegated to the more menial and lower-paying jobs."

According to Howard Glickstein, director of the Center for Civil Rights at the University of Notre Dame, the need for the inclusion of colleges and universities within the coverage of the Equal Employment Act was illustrated by the extent to which charges of discrimination have been filed with the EEOC. In 1973, he said, approximately one out of four EEOC charges involved higher education. "While a charge is not proof..., I believe that the large number of charges filed against educational institutions in the short time they have been covered by the act is indicative of a widespread and pervasive problem."[15]

[14] *Contractors Association of Eastern Pennsylvania* v. *Secretary of Labor*, 442 F 2d 159 (3d Cir. 1971).
[15] "Discrimination in Higher Education: A Debate on Faculty Employment," *Civil Rights Digest*, spring 1975, p. 12.

In addition to coping with charges of discrimination in employment, colleges and universities also were under heavy pressure to increase the number of women and minority students, particularly in graduate and professional schools.[16] To meet these demands most schools adopted preferential admissions programs, favoring minority group members.

Among the schools adopting a preferential admissions policy was the University of Washington. In 1971 its law school received 1,600 applications for 150 openings that September. Among the applicants rejected was Marco DeFunis, a white Phi Beta Kappa graduate of the university's undergraduate program. Among those admitted were 36 minority-group students whose grades and law school admission test scores were lower than those of DeFunis. The law school acknowedged that minority applicants had been judged separately. DeFunis sued, charging that he had been deprived of his constitutional right to equal protection under the law.

A trial court in Seattle agreed and ordered the school to enroll him. The university complied but appealed and the state supreme court, in 1973, ruled in favor of the school. DeFunis then appealed to the U.S. Supreme Court, and Justice William O. Douglas granted a stay that permitted him to remain in school pending a Supreme Court decision. But the Court, by a 5-4 vote on April 23, 1974, refused to decide the case—on the ground that the question was moot because DeFunis had been attending school and was expected to graduate within two months.

The Court's action was anti-climactic in a case which had produced substantial advance publicity. Some 64 organizations spoke up on the issue in 26 "friend of the court" briefs submitted to the Court. Among those submitting briefs supporting DeFunis were the Anti-Defamation League of B'nai B'rith, the Joint Civic Action Committee of Italian Americans, the Advocate Society (a Polish-American lawyers' association), the AFL-CIO, the National Association of Manufacturers and the U.S. Chamber of Commerce. Briefs defending the university were submitted by the former deans of the Yale and Harvard law schools, Louis Pollak and Erwin Griswold, the American Bar Association, the National Urban Coalition and a number of educational institutions, including the national associations of both law schools and medical schools.

Justice Douglas, one of the four dissenting justices, submitted a separate 29-page opinion in which he sharply criticized preferential admissions policies. Each application should be considered in a racially neutral way, Douglas emphasized: "A

---

[16] See "Blacks on Campus," *E.R.R.,* 1972 Vol. II, pp. 667-684.

DeFunis who is white is entitled to no advantage by reason of that fact; nor is he subject to any disability.... Whatever his race he had a constitutional right to have his application considered on its individual merits in a racially neutral manner."

But Douglas went on to say that schools should not have to judge applicants solely on the basis of their grades or test scores. A black applicant "who pulled himself out of the ghetto into a junior college...," Douglas wrote, "may thereby demonstrate a level of motivation, perseverance and ability that would lead a fair-minded admissions committee to conclude that he shows more promise for law study than the son of a rich alumnus who received better grades at Harvard."

Complaint Investigations and Leading Decisions

The Equal Employment Opportunity Commission was created by the 1964 Civil Rights Act to investigate employment discrimination complaints. In 1972, upon passage of the Equal Opportunity Act, the commission gained authority to bring civil suits directly against employers it found to be engaging in discriminatory practices. The EEOC's impact on American business has been characterized in a law journal in the following way:

> The period from 1964 to 1974 marked a major change not only in the composition of the national work force, but, perhaps more importantly, in the attitudes and personnel policies of those involved in the labor market. It was a decade in which employment expectations and opportunities of...blacks and women were expanded greatly. Employers and unions were forced to reconsider carefully their standards for hiring, promotion and membership.[17]

In most instances, change did not come easily or voluntarily. Most cases required court action. Some of the leading cases were these:

> Anaconda Aluminum Co. in 1971 was ordered to pay $190,000 in back wages and court costs to 276 women who alleged that the company maintained sex-segregated job classifications.

> Virginia Electric Power Co. in 1971 was ordered to pay $250,000 to compensate black workers for wages they would have earned if they had not been denied promotion by a discriminatory system. The company also was told that one-fourth of the new employees in union jobs should be non-white.

> Black employees of the Lorillard Corp. were awarded $500,000 in back pay in 1971 by a court that found contracts between the company and its union limited access of blacks to most jobs. The company and union were ordered to assure that blacks had equal opportunity for assignment and promotion in all jobs.

---

[17] "The Second Decade of Title VII: Refinement of the Remedies," *William and Mary Law Review*, spring 1975, p. 436.

The Household Finance Corp. was ordered in 1972 to pay more than $125,000 to women employees who charged that they were denied promotions because of their sex. HFC also agreed to train women and minority employees for better jobs.

The American Telephone & Telegraph Co., in one of the most important of all affirmative action settlements, agreed in January 1973 to open thousands of jobs to women and minority groups, and to pay $15-million in back wages for past discrimination *(see box, p. 45)*.

The government won a significant victory in June 1974 when the Supreme Court ruled[18] that employers must pay men and women equal pay for what is essentially equal work. Under the ruling, Corning Glass Works of New York was ordered to pay approximately $500,000 in back pay to women who had been receiving a lower base salary for daytime work than men who did similar jobs at night. That same month the Bank of America reached an out-of-court settlement of a class-action suit filed on behalf of its women employees. Bank of America agreed (1) to pay an estimated $10-million in compensatory salary increases for its women employees, (2) to set up a $3.75-million trust fund for education and "self-development" programs for women employees, and (3) to increase the over-all proportion of women officers to 40 per cent by 1978, up from 18 per cent.

Merrill Lynch, Pierce, Fenner & Smith, the country's biggest securities firm, settled two separate but related bias suits on June 4, 1976, when it agreed to pay $1.9-million in back pay awards to women and minorities affected by alleged discriminatory hiring and promotion practices. Merrill Lynch also agreed to spend $1.3-million on a five-year affirmation action plan designed to recruit more women and minority employees.

Controversy Over Seniority Rights

E MPLOYMENT OPPORTUNITIES for women and minorities expanded rapidly between 1964 and 1973. By 1974, however, the situation had begun to change. The United States entered an economic recession and employers, both public and private, began to lay off workers, often using the long-accepted principle of "last hired, first-fired," whereby workers who lacked seniority were laid off first.

Fearing that this practice would erode the improvements in minority and female employment of the preceding years, civil rights advocates tried to outlaw the use of straight seniority

---

[18] *Corning Glass Works v. Brennan*, 427 U.S. 188.

systems, arguing that they perpetuated the effects of past discrimination. If women and minorities had not previously been discriminated against, it was said, they would have have an opportunity to build up more seniority. Minorities "are being penalized twice," said Herbert Hill of the NAACP, "once by not being hired, and now once they are hired, by being laid off first."[19] To remedy this situation and protect the job gains of women and minorities, some persons suggested a system of "artificial" or "retroactive" seniority dating from the time the employee originally was turned down for a job.[20]

Defenders of the "last in—first out" principle argued that it was a non-discriminatory way of dealing with job losses. Moreover, they said, granting seniority to someone who had not earned it amounted to reverse discrimination. The concept of "fictional" seniority is alien to American jurisprudence, said William Kilberg, a Department of Justice attorney.[21] Union officials said that seniority was too important to the daily lives of workers to be compromised. It affects not only layoff and rehiring policies, but promotions, vacations, transfers, overtime distribution, job assignments and even parking space. Often eligibility for pensions or profit sharing is related to length of service. Finally, pro-seniority forces pointed out, the 1964 Civil Rights Act upholds a "bona fide" seniority system.

> Title VII, section 703 (h) states: "[I]t shall not be an unlawful employment practice for an employer to apply different standards of compensation, or different terms, conditions or privileges of employment pursuant to a bona fide seniority or merit system...provided that such differences are not the result of an intention to discriminate because of race, color, religion, sex or national origin..."

> Title VII, section 703 (j) states: "Nothing contained in this title shall be interpreted to require any employer...to grant preferential treatment to any individual or to any group because of the race, color, religion, sex or national origin of such individual or group on account of an imbalance which may exist with respect to the total number or percentage of persons of any race, color, religion, sex or national origin employed by any employer..."

Supreme Court Ruling on Retroactive Seniority
Though the lower courts have split on the question of fictional seniority, the Supreme Court offered some clarification of the issue on March 24, 1976. It upheld the right to award seniority

---

[19] Quoted in "Last Hired, First Fired—Latest Recession Headache," *U.S. News & World Report*, April 7, 1975, p. 74.
[20] See Michael J. Hogan, "Artificial Seniority for Minorities As a Remedy for Past Bias vs. Seniority Rights of Nonminorities," *University of San Francisco Law Review*, fall 1974, pp. 344-359; Michael Joseph, "Retroactive Seniority—The Courts as Personnel Director," *Oklahoma Law Review*, winter 1976, pp. 215-223; and Donald R. Stacy, "Title VII Seniority Remedies in a Time of Economic Downturn" *Vanderbilt Law Review*, April 1975, pp. 487-520.
[21] Quoted by Bertrand B. Pogrebin, "Who Shall Work?" *Ms.*, December 1975, p. 71.

rights retroactively to persons who could prove they would have been hired earlier had they not suffered from illegal racial or sexual discrimination. Thus if a woman or a black had been rejected for a job in, say, 1970, and was finally hired in 1973, he or she today would be entitled to six years seniority instead of three.

The ruling came in a case brought by two black men—Harold Franks and Johnnie Lee—against Bowman Transportation Co. in Atlanta. Franks, a Bowman employee, had been denied a promotion because of his race. Lee was refused a driver's job on the same basis. Lower courts found clear evidence of illegal discrimination, and ordered the company to remedy its actions—but refused to go as far as to order the company to award Franks and Lee retroactive seniority.

The Supreme Court disagreed. Justice William J. Brennan, author of the majority opinion, asserted that if the person merely was awarded a job he should have had, he "will never obtain his rightful place in the hierarchy of seniority...He will perpetually remain subordinate to persons who, but for the illegal discrimination, would have been...his inferiors." Chief Justice Warren E. Burger, one of the three dissenting justices, said awards of retroactive seniority at the expense of other employees were rarely fair. "I cannot join in judicial approval of 'robbing Peter to pay Paul,' " he said. Burger suggested that victims of such discrimination be given a monetary award in lieu of the seniority grant. AFL-CIO Special Counsel Larry Gold said the ruling provided "full remedy to employees who have actually suffered from discrimination."[22] But at the same time labor spokesmen reiterated their opposition to any effort to undermine the basic principles of seniority systems.

Layoffs or Worksharing: A Search for Alternatives

The Franks case still leaves a number of questions unanswered. The ruling applies only to applicants who can prove they were victims of discrimination. What about persons who never bothered to apply for jobs because they were aware of a company's long history of discrimination? Are they entitled to fictional seniority also? Nor did the ruling resolve the "last hired—first fired" controversy. The Court currently is reviewing several petitions to hear cases seeking to abolish seniority systems that would affect a disproportionate number of minority and female workers in a layoff situation. Pro-seniority forces hope the Court follows the example of U.S. Appeals Court Judge Leonard I. Garth of Philadelphia who, in a case involving Jersey Central Power and Light Co., ruled in February 1975 that anti-discrimination goals cannot take precedence over workers'

---

[22] Quoted in *Time*, April 5, 1976, p. 65.

seniority rights in layoffs without a specific mandate from Congress.

Some companies are searching for alternatives to seniority-based layoffs. Some possibilities were discussed in February 1975 at a conference sponsored by the New York City Commission on Human Rights. One suggestion was to reduce the hours worked by all employees. This could be accomplished in several ways: shutting down the plant or office for a specified time per month, adopting a shorter workweek or workday, eliminating overtime, encouraging voluntary leaves of absence or early retirement. Employees also could be encouraged to accept voluntary wage cuts and deferral of raises, bonuses and cost-of-living increases. Furthermore, employers should determine if they could cut costs, other than wages, without interfering with plant operations or harming the position of minorities and women.

If layoffs were unavoidable, they could be made on a rotating basis so that each employee could work part of the time. This would spread the layoff burden among all employees rather than concentrating it among the newly hired. Another plan discussed at the New York conference was that of laying off newly hired women and minorities in the same proportion as the over-all layoff. For instance, if 10 per cent of the work force must be dismissed, just 10 per cent of the low-seniority women and minorities would lose their jobs. A few companies are even experimenting with "inverse seniority," which requires older employees who have accumulated high unemployment benefits—such as union-negotiated supplemental unemployment payments—to bear the brunt of layoffs.

Most people agree that the best solution to the layoff problem is full employment. But until that goal is reached the courts will have to determine where the rights of women and minorities end and where those of whites and males begin.

Selected Bibliography

Books

Glazer, Nathan, *Affirmative Discrimination: Ethnic Inequality and Public Policy,* Basic Books, 1975.

O'Neil, Robert M., *Discriminating Against Discrimination: Preferential Admissions and the DeFunis Case,* Indiana University Press, 1975.

Articles

Bennett, Ralph Kinney, "Colleges Under the Federal Gun," *Readers Digest,* May 1976.

Civil Rights Digest, spring 1975 issue.

Davis, Bernard D., "Academic Standards in Medical Schools," *The New England Journal of Medicine,* May 13, 1976.

Edwards, Harry T. and Barry L. Zaretsky, "Preferential Remedies for Employment Discrimination," *Michigan Law Review,* November 1975.

Egan, Richard, "Atonement Hiring," *The National Observer,* July 3, 1976.

Foster, J.W., "Race and Truth at Harvard," *The New Republic,* July 17, 1976.

Hechinger, Fred M., "Justice Douglas's Dissent in the DeFunis Case," *Saturday Review/World,* July 27, 1974.

Hook, Sidney and Miro Todorovich, "The Tyranny of Reverse Discrimination," *Change,* winter 1975-1976.

Joseph, Michael, "Retroactive Seniority—The Court as Personnel Director," *Oklahoma Law Review,* winter 1976.

Pogrebin, Bertrand B., "Who Shall Work?" *Ms.,* December 1975.

Society, January-February 1976 issue.

Stewart, Shirley E., "The Myth of Reverse Race Discrimination," *Cleveland State Law Review,* Vol. 23, 1974.

Thurow, Lester C., "The Economic Status of Minorities and Women," *Civil Rights Digest,* winter/spring 1976.

Virginia Law Review, October 1974 issue.

William and Mary Law Review, spring 1975 issue.

"Court Turning Against Reverse Discrimination," *U.S. News & World Report,* July 12, 1976.

"More Seniority for the Victims," *Time,* April 5, 1976.

"Racism in Reverse," *Newsweek,* March 11, 1974.

"Reverse Discrimination—Has It Gone Too Far?" *U.S. News & World Report,* March 29, 1976.

Reports and Studies

Editorial Research Reports, "Black Americans, 1963-1973," 1973 Vol. II, p. 623; "Blacks on Campus," 1972 Vol. II, p. 667; "Future of Private Colleges," 1976 Vol. I, p. 305.

U.S. Bureau of the Census, "The Social and Economic Status of the Black Population in the United States, 1974."

U.S. Department of Labor, "1975 Handbook on Women Workers."

U.S. Equal Employment Opportunity Commission, "Affirmative Action and Equal Employment: A Guidebook for Employers," January 1974.

S INGLE-PARENT FAMILIES

by

Sandra Stencel

Sept. 10
1 9 7 6

SINGLE-PARENT FAMILIES

T HE PROBLEMS of the American family and what the government can do toward solving them have become a popular theme in this year's presidential campaign. Typical of his comments about home and family, Democratic candidate Jimmy Carter told a group of supporters in Manchester, N.H., on Aug. 3: "There can be no more urgent priority for the next administration than to see that every decision our government makes is designed to honor and support and strengthen the American family." The Republican Party Platform, adopted in Kansas City two weeks later, expressed similar sentiments. "It is imperative," the Republicans stated, "that our government's programs, actions, officials and social welfare institutions never be allowed to jeopardize the family."

Policies of the federal government relating to the family traditionally have been geared to the needs of the two-parent or nuclear family, with a working father, a homemaking mother and dependent children. Only recently has the government begun to respond to the actual and growing variety of American family lives, including the tremendous growth in the number of families headed by women who work. One of the most significant changes in family structure in recent years has been the increase in the number of children living with only one parent. Over 11 million children—more than one out of every six children under age 18—live in single-parent homes. Since 1960 the number of such families has grown seven times as fast as the number of two-parent families. By 1975, there were 4.9 million one parent families in the United States—up from 3.26 million in 1970.[1]

Most Americans raising their children alone are women. Of the 4.9 million single-parent families, 4.4 million were headed by women.[2] The number of children living in homes where the father was absent more than doubled from 1960 to 1975. Today, approximately 15 per cent of all families with children under 18 are headed by single mothers. This trend has been particularly

---

[1] U.S. Bureau of the Census, "Household and Family Characteristics: March 1975," *Current Population Reports,* Series P-20, No. 291, February 1976, p. 7.
[2] The tendency to use figures on families headed by women as indicators of characteristics of families headed by single mothers can be somewhat misleading since not all households headed by women have children living at home. Of the seven million households headed by women in 1975, approximately two-thirds had children under 18.

pronounced among black families—more than 40 per cent of all black children live in homes where the father is absent. Behind this growth in one-parent families is the explosive rise in the divorce rate, which doubled in the past decade. There were over one million divorces in the United States in 1975—a record high. If the current divorce rate continues, three out of every five couples who marry this year will not remain together.

The rapid growth in the number of single-parent families is a source of concern among some social scientists, child psychologists and public officials. Many view the trend as evidence of the breakup of the American family. "Profound changes are taking place in the lives of America's children and young people," writes Urie Bronfenbrenner, professor of human development and family studies at Cornell University. "The institution which is at the center of these changes and that itself shows the most rapid and radical transformation is the American family...."[3]

Another expert troubled by the increase in one-parent families is Dr. Herbert Hendin, director of psychosocial studies at the Center for Policy Research and a professor at Columbia University. "As a culture we encourage the forces that are pulling the family apart...," he wrote recently in *The New York Times*. "A well-functioning culture can tolerate many individual alternatives to family life. But our effort should not be to institutionalize such alternatives; rather, we should help men and women to make their families work."[4]

Not everyone views the increase in single-parent families with alarm. Carole Klein, author of *The Single Parent Experience* (1973), suggests that the United States is in the midst of a significant change in child-rearing patterns. "The story of the single parent is the story of a growing, if grudging, acceptance of variations on our most treasured theme. Like every other aspect of our culture, the family as we knew it is in transition. We are rethinking assumptions on which generations of people have lived, and finding that they were after all only assumptions. For some people, this is terribly exciting. It opens up a tremendous range of possibilities for behavior."

Other social scientists contend that the growth of single-parent families should not be viewed as a rejection of marriage or family living. They cite statistics indicating that half of these one-parent families are likely to evolve into new nuclear families within five years. "We need to recognize that single parenting is not a static category but rather a state of transition," said Martin Rein, a sociologist at the Massachusetts Institute of

---

[3] Urie Bronfenbrenner, *The Origins of Alienation* (1975).
[4] *The New York Times*, Aug. 26, 1976.

15% of all families with children are headed by women

4.4 million of the 4.9 million single-parent families in U.S. are headed by women

11% of all white children live in homes where the father is absent

41% of all black children live in homes where the father is absent

Technology in a research paper on single-parent families prepared for the U.S. Office of Child Development in 1974.[5] This transitory theme is echoed in a recent report on the growth of families headed by women prepared by Urban Institute economists Heather L. Ross and Isabel V. Sawhill. For most people, they write, "single parenthood is a 'time of transition' between living in one nuclear family and another."[6]

Increased Child Adoptions by Single Persons

In recent years, those men and women who become single parents through death or divorce have been joined by a small but growing number who have freely chosen this role. Some single persons decided to adopt children. Some unmarried

[5] Hugh Helco, Lee Rainwater, Martin Rein and Robert Weiss, "Single Parent Families: Issues and Policies," unpublished manuscript, 1974.
[6] Heather L. Ross and Isabel V. Sawhill, "Time of Transition: The Growth of Families Headed by Women," The Urban Institute, 1975, p. 159.

women deliberately became pregnant, often without ever letting the man know he was the father. Others accidentally conceived and decided to go through with the pregnancy even though marriage with the baby's father was not likely. According to Carole Klein, well over half of the single pregnant women who contact social service agencies are deciding to keep their babies rather than give them up for adoption. "If this cannot yet be called a trend," she wrote, "it certainly indicates a shift in some of our most entrenched social attitudes."

Statistics on the number of single persons who have become adoptive parents are vague, but according to Betsy Cole, director of the North American Center for Adoption of the Child Welfare League of America, "there are more single parents today than in the entire history of adoption." In the past, single parents were chosen only for youngsters no one else wanted. Today, however, single adults are actually sought out for many children. "In many cases, particularly with older children, there may be a better emotional relationship with just one parent," said Lenore K. Campbell, director of Los Angeles Adoptions.[7] Nevertheless, some professionals continue to oppose single-parent adoptions. Dr. Lee Salk, a leading child psychologist, wrote recently: "I always wonder if people who deliberately choose to be single parents are thinking of the child or are trying to satisfy some hidden self-interest."[8]

Money Problems of Families Headed by Women

As the number of single-parent families has increased, Americans have become increasingly aware of the multitude of legal, financial, emotional and social problems that confront this growing minority. The great majority of one-parent families face severe economic handicaps. Often single parents start off with sizable debts, the result of costly divorce proceedings or medical treatment for a now-deceased spouse. Divorced couples quickly discover that two cannot live as cheaply as one. As a result, both households are forced to reduce their living standard.

Generally, economic problems are greatest for single mothers. The income of single-parent families headed by women is much lower than of those headed by men *(see box, p. 674)*. In 1974, over half (51.5 per cent) of all children living in families headed by women were living below the official poverty level.[9] For black children living with single mothers, this figure was even higher—almost two-thirds (65.7 per cent) were living in poverty.

One factor contributing to the poverty of families headed by

---

[7] Cole and Campbell were quoted in *The Christian Science Monitor*, Dec. 22, 1975.

[8] Dr. Lee Salk, "Guilt and the Single Parent," *Harper's Bazaar*, March 1976, p. 89.

[9] In 1974 the official federal poverty line for a non-farm family of four was $5,038; for · family of five, $5,950; for a family of six, $6,699.

single mothers is the number of fathers who default on their child-support payments. On the basis of a much-cited study conducted by the University of Wisconsin in the 1950s, it is estimated that four of every ten divorced fathers are not paying any child support one year after the divorce. After ten years, eight of the ten make no support payments. Non-support is as prevalent among affluent and middle-class fathers as among low-income men, according to a research paper published by the Rand Corporation in 1974.[10]

Data collected by the General Accounting Office in 1974 also indicate that there is little relationship between a father's ability to pay and either the amount of the payment agreed to or his compliance with the law. While some low-income men are paying substantial portions of their income to support their children, many who are more affluent have failed to comply at all.[11] A study by Robert Hampton of the University of Michigan's Institute for Social Research portrays ex-wives as being worse off financially than ex-husbands. Of all the married couples in his survey who separated between 1968 and 1973, 35 per cent of the women but only 19 per cent of the men fell into the botton 30 per cent of the nation's income brackets after being divorced.[12]

The federal government has opened a campaign to track down negligent fathers and make them pay for their children's support *(see p. 674)*. The government hopes that better enforcement of child-support orders will reduce the number of single-parent families on welfare. The number of single mothers who are dependent on public largesse is smaller than is commonly

---

[10] Marian P. Winston and Trude Forsher, "Nonsupport of Legitimate Children by Affluent Fathers as a Cause of Poverty and Welfare Dependence," the Rand Corporation, April 1974.

[11] *Congressional Record*, Dec. 4, 1974.

[12] These figures took into account family size and any child support or alimony obligations. See *Five Thousand Families—Patterns of Economic Progress*, Vols. 1-3, Institute for Social Research, University of Michigan, 1973-1975.

believed. According to the U.S. Office of Child Development research paper, only 35 per cent of all families headed by mothers receive welfare aid; no more than 20 per cent receive half of their income from welfare; and no more than 10 per cent get as much as three-quarters of their income from welfare.

Most single mothers support themselves and their families with their earnings. The Women's Bureau of the Department of Labor reported that in 1975 some 62 per cent of these mothers held paying jobs; among other mothers, only 43 per cent were employed.[13] Many of these women enter the job market untrained or after a long absence, and are forced to take low-paying jobs as office workers, waitresses or sales clerks. The median income of single working mothers in 1975 was $6,575—substantially below the $13,675 median income of two-parent families in which the husband worked but the wife did not.

A major expense for most single parents—men and women—is day care for their children. This is particularly true for single-parent families that fail to qualify for federally subsidized care for their children *(see p. 675)*. Private day-care centers often charge from $20 to $50 a week per child. Even if a parent has the money, day-care facilities are hard to find. According to the latest government estimates, care in licensed centers is available for only slightly more than one million children. It is estimated that more than six million pre-school children and several million school-age children need this service. Some children of working mothers are cared for by friends or relatives. Some stay with babysitters. Others—"latchkey children"—care for themselves.

Emotional and Social Issues in Single Parenting

Many of the problems single parents face initially are related to the event which led to their new social status—divorce, separation or the death of a spouse. "The end of a marriage, especially if children are involved, is for most people a traumatic experience," said George B. Williams, executive director of Parents Without Partners. "Even if problems are anticipated, nobody ever expects them to be so critical. The frequent responses are demoralization and despair."[14] Many single parents suffer from loneliness. They find that they no longer fit in with their married friends and they learn that it is sometimes difficult to meet members of the opposite sex. Single parents "don't seem to fit any of the normal social patterns," Professor Benjamin Schlesinger of the University of Toronto has observed. "They are the self-styled fifth wheels of society."[15]

---

[13] U.S. Department of Labor, "1975 Handbook on Women Workers," p. 25.
[14] Quoted in "Rising Problems of 'Single Parents,' " *U.S. News & World Report,* July 16, 1973, p. 32.
[15] Benjamin Schlesinger, *The One-Parent Family* (1975), p. 9.

In the case of divorce or separation, problems are apt to arise with the former or absent spouse. Financial arrangements between the couple frequently cause intense conflict. Most often the problems center on the children. A frequent complaint of divorced fathers is that their ex-wives prevent them from seeing their children as often as they would like. On the other hand, the parent with custody often feels burdened by the full responsibility for the children and resents the apparent freedom of the other parent.

Child-care problems do not end once a suitable babysitter is found or the child is enrolled in day care. There are vacations to contend with, school conferences to attend, days when the child is sick, the race to get home before the day-care center closes, the question of what to do with older children before and after school. These problems confront all working parents. But they can be doubly hard on single parents who have no one else to share responsibility for decision making and discipline, no one else to help with the household chores, no one else to give the children the love and attention they need. Under such pressures many single parents develop ambivalent feelings about their children. They may feel their children are a burden to them, interfering with their jobs, their social lives and even their chances of remarriage.

One of the more startling developments in recent years has been the growing number of broken families in which neither parent wants custody. "It's a critical problem," according to Judge John R. Evans of Denver, "and it's definitely increasing."[16] The dread of getting stuck with the children may even be holding some marriages together, *Newsweek* has commented. The magazine said a Chicago divorce lawyer told of a couple who had entered into a written agreement which stipulated that the first one to ask for a divorce had to take the kids. Despite the many difficulties, family counselors stress, most single parents still manage to raise their children successfully.

American Families in Transition

T HE SHARP INCREASE in one-parent families parallels other changes in the structure of American families. Marriages have been occurring later and less often. The age at which young couples get married has been rising since the 1950s. Many single persons are delaying marriage in favor of additional

---

[16] Quoted in "The Broken Family: Divorce U.S. Style," *Newsweek*, March 12, 1973, p. 51.

Living Arrangements of Children Under 18

Living With	1975			1970		
	Total	White	Black	Total	White	Black
Both parents	80.3%	85.4%	49.4%	84.9%	89.2%	58.1%
Mother only	15.5	11.3	40.9	10.7	7.8	29.3
Father only	1.5	1.5	1.8	1.1	0.9	2.2
Neither parent	2.7	1.7	7.9	3.3	2.2	10.4

SOURCE: U.S. Bureau of the Census

schooling and a period of living away from home prior to marriage. Others are living together without the benefit of marriage. In 1975 the average age at marriage—23.5 for males and 21.1 for women—was close to a year higher than it had been in the mid-1950s. Since 1960 the proportion of women who remained single until their early twenties had increased by one-third.[17]

The postponement of marriage, along with the availability of contraceptives and legal abortions, has contributed to a marked decline in childbearing. Young couples today are not having their first child as soon after marriage as their parents did, are spacing the children farther apart and are sharply reducing the number of large families. The total fertility rate[18] among American women in 1975 has been estimated at 1.9, almost half the 1960 figure (3.7) and well below the 1970 figure (2.5). If the estimate proves to be correct, and the rate does not rise again, the national population growth will cease and then decline—unless immigration fills the gap.[19]

The single most important factor contributing to the growth in one-parent families is the rising divorce rate. Social scientists anticipate even higher rates in the future. Dr. Richard A. Gardner, assistant clinical professor of child psychiatry at Columbia University and author of *The Boys and Girls Book About Divorce* (1970), has said: "Today, easier divorce laws and having the economic capacity for an independent existence make it easier for couples to contemplate divorce. The lessening of religion's influence is a factor, too. Furthermore, a kind of cycle develops in these things. Having divorced parents makes it easier for youngsters to get divorces because it's in their scheme of things."[20]

---

[17] U.S. Bureau of the Census, "Some Recent Changes in American Families," *Current Population Reports*, Series P-23, No. 52, 1975.
[18] The average number of births expected during a woman's childbearing life span, arbitrarily determined for statistical purposes as ages 15-44. The *general* fertility rate, in contrast, is the number of babies born per year relative to the number of women aged 15-44. The *birth rate* is the number of children born each year per 1,000 general population.
[19] See "Zero Population Growth," *E.R.R.*, 1971 Vol. II, pp. 903-924.
[20] Quoted in *U.S. News & World Report*, Oct. 27, 1975.

Children are no longer the deterrent to divorce that they used to be. As divorce has become a more common and increasingly acceptable event, the pressure to stay together for the sake of the children has lessened considerably. All of this has produced a shift in the living arrangements of children. Census figures indicate that during the 1960s the number of children living with only one parent increased 12 times as rapidly as children living with both parents. During that decade, the absolute increase in numbers of children in single-parent homes exceeded the increase in children in two-parent homes. Furthermore, this increase occurred among whites as well as blacks.

Government Support of Traditional Family Life

The government was slow to respond to these changes in the American family. Well into the 1970s, according to Louise Kapp Howe, the white, middle-class family with a male breadwinner and female homemaker remained the model against which all who lived differently were judged deviant. Despite the huge numbers of working mothers, of single-parent homes, of youth in communes, and unemployed fathers, she wrote, the government, in practically all its policies related to the family, continued to act as if there were one and only one worthy way to run a household.[21]

In this vein, a report issued by the Department of Labor's Office of Policy Planning and Research in 1965 argued that the black family was "deteriorating" because about a fourth of the black families did not have a male at the head. The report noted:

> Nearly a quarter of urban Negro marriages are dissolved; nearly one-quarter of Negro births are now illegitimate; as a consequence, almost one-fourth of Negro families are headed by females, and this breakdown of the Negro family has led to a startling increase in welfare dependency.

The report, "The Negro Family: The Case for National Action," prepared under the direction of Daniel Patrick Moynihan, the sociologist and author who has held high posts in the Johnson, Nixon and Ford administrations, concluded that only concerted planning and action directed to a new kind of national goal—establishment of a stable black family structure—could forestall "a new crisis in race relations."[22]

Six years later, on Dec. 9, 1971, President Richard Nixon vetoed a bill that would have expanded the government's role in

---

[21] Louise Kapp Howe, ed., *The Future of the Family* (1972), pp. 11-13.

[22] The report was issued in March 1965, intended solely as an internal policy paper. It was made public in August 1965 after some of its contents had been leaked to newsmen. Its release to the public generated a storm of controversy. A detailed account of the genesis of the report and ensuing controversy were the subject of a book published in the spring of 1967, *The Moynihan Report and the Politics of Controversy* (Massachusetts Institute of Technology Press) by sociologists Lee Rainwater and William L. Yancey.

providing child care because of its "family weakening implications." Nixon said the bill "would commit the vast moral authority of the national government to the side of communal approaches to child rearing against the family-centered approach." Furthermore, he said, the bill would impede the government's most important task: "to cement the family in its rightful role as the keystone of our civilization." The persistence of the traditional view of the family was addressed in a discussion of child care alternatives in a 1972 Brookings Institution study of federal budget priorities.

> Decisions about day care and early childhood programs are likely to provoke a heated national debate over the next few years [the Brookings authors wrote], not only because the budgetary consequences might be large, but because sensitive emotional issues are involved. How should the responsibility for children be divided between the family and society? Should mothers of small children work? The spectrum of views is wide....
>
> Traditionally in the United States, the responsibility for the care and supervision of children has rested squarely with parents. Only when a child reached age six did society at large take a major stand by insisting that he attend school.... What happens to the child the rest of the time is his parents' business. Society intervenes only if he is severely abused or neglected or runs afoul of the law.[23]

Public prejudice has been particularly strong against single-parent families. "On the whole, in our society, the one-parent family has been viewed as a form of un-family or sick family," wrote Elizabeth Herzog and Cecilia E. Sudia. "For a number of reasons it would be wiser to recognize the one-parent family as a form that exists and functions...such families can be cohesive, warm, supportive and favorable to...[child] development."[24]

Concern for Children in Family Disorganization

The possibility that the single parent-child arrangement could conceivably be another legitimate form of the family is something the government has been reluctant to admit. This reluctance is linked to the traditional view that children are more likely to grow up to be law-abiding, healthy and happy adults if they spend their entire childhood with both parents than if the family unit is broken by death or divorce. "It has long and widely been thought that [the one-parent family] is damaging to children—not only when they are young but also later in their adult life—and that this, in turn, hurts society, which must cope with the damaged childrens' anti-social behavior or impaired abilities to achieve."[25]

[23] Charles L. Schultze, et al., "Child Care," *Setting National Priorities: The 1973 Federal Budget* (1972), pp. 252-290.

[24] Elizabeth Herzog and Cecilia E. Sudia, "Boys in Fatherless Families," Department of Health, Education, and Welfare reprint, 1972.

[25] Ross and Sawhill, *op. cit.*, p. 132.

Sociologists have traditionally linked broken homes with juvenile delinquency. Their thinking is this: Children from broken homes, boiling with anger and resentment over the loss of a parent—usually the father, thus leaving them without a father's guidance and discipline—can succumb to anti-social behavior such as bullying, truancy, vandalism or worse.[26]

Other experts maintain that delinquency cannot be blamed solely on the lack of a second parent in a home. One study concluded that the onset of delinquency in children from broken homes cannot be attributed to the absence of a parent, but rather to "certain parental characteristics—intense conflict, rejection, and deviance—which occur more commonly in broken families."[27] Many studies have found that children living with unhappily married parents are more likely to get into trouble than children whose parents have little conflict or children in single-parent families.

The emotional impact of divorce on children is a major concern of many single parents. Psychiatrists tend to agree that divorce itself does not necessarily cause psychiatric problems to develop in children. One recent study found that children from one-parent families were under the greatest stress when (1) relations between the parents continued to be turbulent following the divorce, or (2) relations with the parent not in the home were forbidden the child. The authors speculate that children in a family headed by a woman suffer not from the father's absence but from maternal deprivation; women who become single parents are forced to spread their energies beyond their prior childrearing tasks.[28]

The Public Policy Implications

THE CHANGES occurring in children's living arrangements present a challenge to public-policy makers. But exactly what policy response is called for is not clear, according to economists Heather L. Ross and Isabel V. Sawhill.

> Should efforts at keeping families together be undertaken; efforts to make female-headed family life less isolated and deprived; or efforts to facilitate remarriage and the formation of new husband-wife families? What acceptable, effective policy devices are there to promote any of these objectives?

[26] See Sheldon and Eleanor Glueck's *Unraveling Juvenile Delinquency* (1951).

[27] Joan McCord, William McCord and Emily Thurber, "Some Effects of Paternal Absence on Male Children," *Journal of Abnormal and Social Psychology*, March 1962, pp. 361-369.

[28] Ruth A. Brandwein et al., "Women and Children Last: The Social Situation of Divorced Mothers and Their Families," *Journal of Marriage and Family*, August 1974, pp. 498-514.

Mean Family Income, 1974

| Age of Head | Husband-Wife Families | Single-Parent Families | |
		Male-Headed	Female-Headed
Under 25	$ 9,931	$10,351	$3,600
25-44	16,118	12,093	6,481
45-64	18,244	13,045	8,438

SOURCE: U.S. Bureau of the Census

The most pressing policy need, they conclude, is to make life less difficult for female-headed families. Furthermore, they say, "some of the policy options in this area—for example, improved day care, social services, and child-support arrangements—are better defined and more within the range of accepted public policy than are devices to influence private decisions on marriage and family."

The biggest problem facing single-mother households is inadequate income. The traditional response to low-family incomes has been welfare, specifically Aid to Families with Dependent Children. This program is federally aided but administered by the individual states which set eligibility requirements and benefit levels. The average monthly payment in 1975 was $212.90, ranging from $50 in Mississippi to $360 in Massachusetts. Total federal, state and local spending for the program reached $8.5-billion in fiscal year 1975. About three-quarters of the recipient families were headed by women.

Many divorced, separated and deserted mothers end up on welfare because their absent husbands fail to make alimony and child-support payments. In an effort to reduce welfare costs, Congress in December 1974 passed a law requiring states and localities to make a vigorous effort to track down absentee fathers of children on public assistance and make them pay.

The law requires each state to set up special offices responsible for searching for the missing parent, establishing paternity of children born out of wedlock, and bringing action to collect support payments. States must have these services in full operation by Jan. 1, 1977, or face the loss of 5 per cent of their federal welfare funds under the Aid to Families with Dependent Children program.[29]

---

[29] The 1974 act authorized the federal government to pay 75 per cent of the cost of state child-support-enforcement programs. However, the following year Congress reduced this share to 50 per cent for states that had begun setting up their own programs by Aug. 1, 1975.

To help the states locate missing parents, the law provided for a central parent-locator service within the U.S. Department of Health, Education, and Welfare. Through the central unit, the states have access to information in federal files, including Social Security, Civil Service, Treasury and Defense Department records. Currently 14 states[30] are linked to the central unit by computers; the rest send in their requests by mail. The government reports that it has found addresses for almost 90 per cent of the persons for whom the states sought information.

Once the recalcitrant parent is found, the states are permitted under the law to use the federal courts to collect support payments. If the parent fails to comply with a court order mandating payment, the Internal Revenue Service is authorized to collect the money in the same way it collects back taxes. Government employees and members of the military forces are subject to paycheck deductions for child support. Families not on welfare may use these collection services for a fee set by the states. The rationale for allowing this use of the service is that it could help reduce future claims on welfare funds.

A welfare mother who cooperates in locating the absentee father receives up to $20 each month the support is collected. The rest of the money is kept by the government to offset welfare payments made that month to the family or to compensate for past welfare payments to the family. Originally, a mother who failed to help locate the absent father was cut off from welfare payments. But Congress in 1975 exempted the mother from this requirement if a state agency determined that the missing father might subject the children to physical harm or harassment.

Child-Care Programs: Debate Over Federal Role

The U.S. Office of Child Development research paper *(see p. 665)* concluded that federal policies aimed at helping single-parent families have been directed almost exclusively toward those on welfare. Day care is an example. This year the federal government is expected to spend $1.2-billion on child-care services. The bulk of the money will be spent on day care for welfare children whose mothers work or receive job training and on the Head Start program which provides pre-school education for children in poverty.

Federal child-care support available to middle and upper-income families is usually indirect—allowing working parents to deduct some child-care expenses from income subject to federal taxation. The Revenue Act of 1971 greatly liberalized child-care deductions. Under that law, persons working full-time and earn-

---

[30] California, Iowa, Massachusetts, Michigan, Minnesota, Nebraska, New Jersey, New York, Pennsylvania, Tennessee, Texas, Washington, New Mexico, North Carolina.

Bachelor Fathers

Men are raising their children alone, either by choice or circumstance, in increasing numbers. By 1975 there were 500,000 bachelor fathers, twice as many as a decade earlier, in the United States. They were caring for nearly one million children under age 18.

Although adoption by single males has contributed to the increase, the main reason is the liberalized attitude of the courts about awarding custody of the children to the father in divorce cases. In the past, fathers had almost no chance of being awarded custody unless they could prove that their wives were unfit mothers. Women still wind up with the children in 90 per cent of the divorce cases, but this percentage is slowly decreasing.

New York, California and Illinois are among those states which have abandoned the "tender years" doctrine—which holds that children generally are better off with their mothers—and amended their laws to specify that either parent can be awarded custody.

ing $18,000 a year or less could deduct up to $200 a month for the care of one child under age 15; up to $300 a month for two children; and up to $400 a month for three or more children. If the adjusted gross income of the couple or individual exceeded $18,000, the deduction was reduced on a sliding scale. After reaching $27,600 no child-care deduction was allowed. The Tax Reduction Act of 1975 raised the income limits for the child-care deduction from $18,000 to $35,000 and from $27,600 to $44,600.

The deduction is a tremendous help to many single parents. But there is one catch. In order to qualify the parent must (1) have custody of the child and (2) be entitled to claim the child as a tax deduction. The parent who has custody of the child for the greater part of the year normally will be entitled to the dependency exemption. However, the non-custodial parent may claim the exemption if (1) he or she contributes at least $600 a year in child support and the separation agreement or divorce decree gives the exemption to the non-custodial parent; or (2) if he or she contributes $1,200 or more a year in child support and the custodial parent cannot clearly show that he or she contributed a greater amount of support.

If the non-custodial parent does claim the child as a tax deduction, neither parent can deduct day-care or babysitting expenses incurred for the child. To remedy this situation, many single parents advocate changes in tax laws to allow divorced or separated parents to split exemptions and child-care deductions, or allow the parent with custody to claim the deduction whether or not he or she claimed the child as a tax exemption. Single parents also support proposals that would make child-care deductions available to part-time workers and to full-time students. Single parents also argue that child-care expenses should be treated as a legitimate business expense rather than a personal expense. The point is often made that if a company or self-employed person can claim a secretary's salary as a business expense, why cannot an employee claim child-care expenses.

Another special concern of single parents is the lack of day-care facilities for school-age children. Nearly 18 million children from ages 6 to 14 need some form of supervision after school hours, according to the National Council of Organizations for Children and Youth.[31] Dr. Edward Zigler of Yale University told the Senate Subcommittee on Children and Youth in September 1973: "Because of our slowness in developing day-care models for school-age children and inducing schools and other institutions to employ such models, we are now witnessing the national tragedy of over one million latchkey children, cared for by no one, with probably an equal number being cared for by siblings who are themselves too young to assume such responsibilities."

A few corporations have set up supervised day-care centers on their premises. Single-parent groups are trying to encourage more employers to take advantage of section 162 (a) of the Internal Revenue Code. The provision allows a company to claim as a business expense whatever it spends to establish and operate day-care programs for the children of employees if it can show that this is done to increase employee morale and productivity.

"It is not inconceivable," said Dr. Ruby Takanishi, assistant professor of early childhood development at the University of California at Los Angeles, "that child care services can join the range of employee benefits now provided, including health and disability insurance, maternity and military leaves, credit unions, retirement plans and recreational facilities."[32] Dr. Urie Bronfenbrenner of Cornell University advocates extending tax incentives to businesses and industries that modify their work schedules so that parents can be home when their children return from school. Most working parents would welcome the flexible work schedules.

Laws on Discrimination Against Single Parents

In the past, single parents—particularly women—frequently complained of discrimination in trying to obtain housing, credit and insurance. "When I got divorced," said Mrs. Diane Meyers, a Houston secretary, "I discovered that I didn't have any credit. I didn't have a car and couldn't get a loan to buy one. I even had

---

[31] National Council of Organizations for Children and Youth, "America's Children 1976," p. 74.

[32] Quoted in *The Single Parent News*, Vol. 1, No. 2, 1976. The publication is issued bimonthly in Santa Monica, Calif.

trouble finding a place to live because apartment owners feared that a divorced woman could not give proper supervision to the children."[33]

In recent years Congress has taken action to correct these ills. In October 1974, it amended the Consumer Credit Protection Act by adding an "Equal Credit Opportunity" provision. This provision, which went into effect Oct. 28, 1975, makes it illegal to consider sex or marital status in determining credit worthiness. The law applies to all credit transactions, including mortgage applications. Title I of the Housing and Community Development Act of 1974 amended the Fair Housing Act of 1968[34] to prohibit sex discrimination in the financing, sale or rental of housing.

In Denver, Colo., a low-income housing development designed specifically for single parents and their children opened in February 1974. Besides low rent, it offers other advantages to the single parent: day-care facilities for pre-school and school-age youngsters; financial counseling by qualified members of the staff; a group therapy program run by the Denver Mental Health Clinic; educational counseling and adult education programs provided by three colleges in the area.[35]

Arrangements for the Joint Custody of Children

One way to ease the burdens of single parenthood—both financial and emotional—is to encourage more shared responsibility by both parents, according to Dr. Lee Salk. "Women have been reluctant to give up the responsibility for fear they'd be looked down upon," he writes. "I think we ought to move to a point where women will be freer to relinquish some responsibilities to males without feeling stigmatized or guilty. This guilt is all part of the motherhood myth. And children are not benefitting by it."[36]

Although women still retain custody of the children in most divorces, a small but growing number of divorced parents are experimenting with a new kind of arrangement—joint custody. The child spends equal time with both parents. In practice the idea takes many forms. Usually both parents live in the same community so that the child's school life and friendships will not be disrupted. In some joint custody arrangements, each parent maintains a home in which the children have their own space and some of their own things. "This way they are not visitors," Emily Jane Goodman writes.[37]

---

[33] Quoted in *U.S. News & World Report,* July 16, 1973, p. 34.
[34] Title VIII of the 1968 Civil Rights Act.
[35] See Ann O'Shea, "Housing for the Single Parent," *McCall's,* June 1975, p. 36.
[36] Dr. Lee Salk, "Problems and Pleasures of the Single Parent," *Harper's Bazaar,* March 1975, p. 77.
[37] Emily Jane Goodman, "Joint Custody," *McCall's,* August 1975, p. 34.

Some parents avoid the constant moving back and forth by alternating custody every six months or so. Still another variation is for the children to remain in the family home and the parents to take turns living there. Joint custody is also construed to mean that the children live with one parent but the other lives very close by and spends considerable time with them every day. So far the courts have not looked too favorably upon joint custody arrangements. Ms. Goodman said: "Judges tend to follow precedent and are likely to regard joint custody as putting the needs of the parents above those of the children." Consequently, most joint custody agreements are arranged privately between the parents.

How do such arrangements affect the children? It's still too early to tell, but according to Marcia Holly, a free-lance writer who has shared custody of her daughter for four years, children living in joint custody arrangements are less likely to feel that they may be abandoned—a common fear among children of divorce. "Abandonment seems less likely to children where there are two parents and two homes that welcome them," she said. "Their dual homes force them to develop more ways of interacting with a variety of people. Most of these children seem to feel pleasurable anticipation about alternating homes rather than resentment or sadness at leaving one house for the other."[38]

Those parents who do retain full custody of their children are looking for other solutions to the problems of single parenthood. In some areas, single parents are forming small collectives that allow them to pool their financial and emotional resources. This arrangement also allows them to share babysitting and housekeeping chores. Other single parents are finding emotional support in informal, extended family arrangements, a concept pioneered by the Unitarian-Universalist Church. Many single parents find that other single parents are their best source of support. Over 80,000 single parents belong to Parents Without Partners, a nationwide organization offering counseling, seminars and social activities for members and their children.

Momma, an organization for single mothers with headquarters in Los Angeles, has about 50 chapters across the country. Its goals are to stimulate research on single motherhood and its impact on the general society, to provide a clearinghouse for resources and information relevant to single mothers, and to assist single mothers in achieving economic self-sufficiency, education and child-rearing guidance. These goals will be easier to achieve as the government becomes more responsive to the needs of this growing minority.

---

[38] Marcia Holly, "Joint Custody: The New Haven Plan," *Ms.*, September 1976, pp. 70-71. See also Elizabeth Dancy, "Who Gets the Kids?" *Ms.*, September 1976, p. 70.

Selected Bibliography

Books

Gardner, Richard A., *The Boys and Girls Book About Divorce*, Bantam Books, 1970.

Howe, Louise Kapp, ed., *The Future of the Family*, Simon & Schuster, 1972.

Kay, F. George, *The Family in Transition*, John Wiley & Sons, 1972.

Ross, Heather L. and Isabel V. Sawhill, *Time of Transition: The Growth of Families Headed By Women*, The Urban Institute, 1975.

Schlesinger, Benjamin, *The One-Parent Family*, University of Toronto Press, 1975.

Yorburg, Betty, *The Changing Family*, Columbia University Press, 1973.

Articles

Dancey, Elizabeth, "Who Gets Custody?" *Ms.*, September 1976.

Holly, Marcia, "Joint Custody: The New Haven Plan," *Ms.*, September 1976.

MacDonald, Steve, "The Alimony Blues," *The New York Times Magazine*, March 16, 1975.

McEaddy, Beverly Johnson, "Women Who Head Families: A Socioeconomic Analysis," *Monthly Labor Review*, June 1976.

Salk, Lee, "Guilt and the Single Parent," *Harper's Bazaar*, March 1976.

____"Problems and Pleasures of the Single Parent," *Harper's Bazaar*, March 1975.

"Rising Problems of 'Single Parents,'" *U.S. News & World Report*, July 16, 1973.

"The Broken Family: Divorce U.S. Style," *Newsweek*, March 12, 1973.

Reports and Studies

"America's Children 1976," National Council of Organizations for Children and Youth, 1976.

Editorial Research Reports, "Marriage: Changing Institution," 1971 Vol. II, p. 759; "Child Care," 1972 Vol. II, p. 439; "Child Support," 1974 Vol. I, p. 61; "No-Fault Divorce," 1973 Vol. II, p. 777.

Helco, Hugh, et al., "Single-Parent Families: Issues and Policies," unpublished draft manuscript, 1974.

Senate Subcommittee on Children and Youth, "American Families: Trends and Pressures 1973," hearings Sept. 24-26, 1973.

U.S. Bureau of the Census, "Female Family Heads," *Current Population Reports*, Series P-23, No. 50, July 1974.

____"Household and Family Characteristics, March 1975," *Current Population Reports*, Series P-20, No. 291, February 1976.

____"Marital Status and Living Arrangements, March 1975," *Current Population Reports*, Series P-20, No. 287, December 1975.

____"Some Recent Changes in American Families," Series P-23, No. 52, 1975.

Winston, Marian P. and Trude Forsher, "Nonsupport of Legitimate Children By Affluent Fathers as a Cause of Poverty and Welfare Dependence," the Rand Corporation, April 1974.

WOMEN IN SPORTS

by

Marc Leepson

May 6
1977

WOMEN IN SPORTS

T HE BELIEF that athletics helps people develop good health and physical fitness has long been held by the vast majority in our society. But until the last few years, sports-conscious America was concerned primarily with men's sports. As a result, women have lagged far behind in every aspect of sports participation, from facilities and coaching to media coverage. Inequities facing women in sports have extended from kindergarten through college, from the public playground through the professional ranks.

There has been some change in the situation in the last few years, primarily as a result of the women's rights movement. One observer has said that the women's movement "made both sexes aware of the huge inequities in every area of work and play, and made it easier for women to demand access to the money, the training and the facilities available to the other sex."[1] Much of the incentive to open new areas in sport to women has come from legal action growing out of existing federal and state laws. The most important government ruling affecting women in sports was based on a provision of the Education Amendments of 1972. Title IX of the Education Amendments states:

> No person in the United States shall, on the basis of sex, be excluded from participation in, be denied the benefits of, or be subject to discrimination under any education program or activity receiving federal financial assistance.

Regulations delineating how Title IX affects athletics were drawn up by the Department of Health, Education and Welfare (HEW), and approved by President Ford on May 27, 1975. The new rules, which went into effect July 21, 1975, gave elementary schools one year to comply with sex-integration regulations for physical education and athletic programs. Secondary and post-secondary institutions were given three years to comply. "Title Nine" has become the catalyst for change in school sports *(see p. 91)*, and indeed the term has entered the everyday language in sports pages and on campuses.

The issue of women in sports is unique and complex, and it reaches well beyond sports. It indicates the way society looks at

---

[1] Ellen Weber, "The Long March," *womenSports*, September 1974, p. 34.

male and female roles. Dorothy Harris, director of the Center for Women and Sport at Pennsylvania State University, has said that the No. 1 problem facing women in sports is the behavior expected of females by society.[2] Many people believe that aggressiveness and physical and mental strength are proper traits for men only; they frown upon the passive male and the aggressive female. These attitudes relate directly to sports. "Women have not been encouraged to participate in athletics at least partly because the traits associated with athletic excellence—achievement, self-confidence, aggressiveness, leadership, strength, swiftness—are often seen as being in 'contradiction' with the role of women," Margaret Dunkle, a leading expert on women in athletics, has written.[3]

Sex-Role Stereotyping and Athletic Ability

The attitude that athletic prowess is desirable for men but not for women has been reinforced in many ways. Many parents discourage their daughters from taking part in strenuous exercise and sports but encourage their sons to take part. Until Title IX was enacted, most elementary schools divided physical education classes by sex. Boys were taught competitive sports like kickball, dodgeball, basketball and baseball. Some contact sports were taught in girls' physical education classes. But many schools encouraged girls to play jacks, hopscotch and jump rope. Until a few years ago, most high schools expected boys to play football and basketball and girls to lead the cheers.

"It's not really the girls' fault if they're not interested in sports," a young woman athlete told a magazine reporter. "It's the teachers' and parents' attitude toward the students that's the problem."[4] In addition to influence from parents and teachers, young people are subject to what many believe is the most intense influence to conform to sex stereotypes: peer-group pressure. Young girls who enjoy participating in competitive sports are called "tomboys." By age 12 or 13 tomboys begin to experience pressure from their friends to stop "acting like boys" and begin dating.

The belief that strenuous physical activity is "unfeminine" gradually is becoming less pervasive. It is not uncommon today to see women taking part in athletic activities such as jogging and bicycle riding. Participation by girls in school sports also is increasing *(see p. 94)*. And as women participate more in sports, myths are being dispelled.

---

[2] Interview, "Will Women Ever Equal Men in Sprts?" a publication by the Pennsylvania State University Department of Public Information, 1976.

[3] Margaret Dunkle, "What Constitutes Equality for Women in Sport?" booklet published by the Project on the Status and Education of Women, September 1975, p. 2.

[4] Quoted by Ellen Weber, "Our Own Worst Enemies," *womenSports*, September 1974, p. 38.

Myths About Women Athletes

- Women are less competitive and aggressive than men.

- Contact sports harm women's reproductive organs and breasts.

- Women cannot regain physical prowess after childbirth.

- Women cannot exert peak athletic performances during menstruation.

- Weight lifting builds large muscles in women.

- Competition in contact sports is not feminine.

- Men are inherently better athletes than women.

One widely held myth is that taking part in contact sports is harmful to a woman's reproductive organs and breasts. Doctors say that there is virtually no risk of harming a woman's sexual organs during physical activity. Dorothy Harris has said that a woman has "more natural protection than a man and her sex organs are internal, making them almost invulnerable to injury." Another myth holds that a woman cannot exert maximum physical strength during menstruation. But world records have been set and Olympic gold medals won by women during all stages of their menstrual cycles.

It also is said that a woman's athletic abilities decline after childbirth. But, again, no evidence has been put forth to prove that allegation. "There is no need to restrict physical activity for women in any manner whatsoever," Joan Gillette, an athletic trainer, told the National Conference on Medical Aspects of Sports last year. "There...are no ill effects during pregnancy, delivery or later on," she said. "Women athletes receive injuries due to the lack of proper conditioning and poor coaching...."[5]

Many persons say that men are inherently better athletes than women. They point out that women's world records in every sport are consistently inferior to men's. It also is argued that males generally are bigger, stronger and more muscular than females. Others contend that the difference in male and female physical abilities is caused not by innate physiological differences, but by social and psychological forces that allow males infinitely better opportunities to develop athletically.

An Australian geneticist, K. F. Dyer, recently completed an examination of the performances of male and female track athletes in 15 countries. He found that women performed better in countries that gave women and men the most equal athletic opportunities. Some female track athletes' best performances came within 10 per cent of the best male efforts. And the best women swimmers trailed the best male swimmers by only 6 per cent. "If these are valid measures of female athletic inferiority," Dyer said, "we can clearly envisage a day when the supreme performances of male and female are likely to be essentially equal, or nearly so, in these track events."[6]

The most important physiological factor determining human athletic ability is the effect of hormones on the physical maturation process. All male and female bodies contain both estrogen, the female hormone, and testosterone, the male hormone. Males have a much higher ratio of testosterone; females a significantly greater amount of estrogen. Boys and girls mature nearly evenly until about age ten. For the next five or six years, girls undergo a rapid physical maturation process. During this time, boys also are maturing, but not as rapidly as girls. Males reach their maximum growth at around age 20. The longer, slower growth in males results primarily in more defined muscles, especially in the upper body and arms. It also is responsible for such sex characteristics as lower voices and facial hair. The rapid female maturation process causes most women to have lower centers of gravity than males because more weight is concentrated in women's thighs and hips. Thus, the only innate advantage men have over women is a stronger upper body.

There is no essential difference between male and female cardiovascular systems, respiratory capacity or metabolism. This means that women are capable of developing athletic skills, such as dexterity, agility and coordination on a par with men.

---

[5] Quoted by the Associated Press in *The Washington Post*, June 27, 1976.

[6] Quoted in "Catch-Up Time for Female Athletes," *Human Behavior*, January 1977, p. 36.

And studies have shown that women can greatly increase their strength through weight lifting. An experiment conducted by Jack Wilmore, head of the department of physical education at the University of Arizona, involved a 10-week weight-training program with a group of untrained college-age men and women. Wilmore found that the women came within 25 per cent of men in leg strength. Related to overall body weight, the male-female leg-strength difference was only 7 per cent. "We've always been told that women are so much weaker than men," Wilmore said. "Here it turns out that they have almost exactly the same leg strength."[7] Wilmore believes that his study shows that biological differences are not the prime determinant in athletic ability.

Even though an increasing number of female athletes are turning to weight training, many women are reluctant to use weights. The fear is that they will develop large, unflattering muscles. But another study by Wilmore showed that women developed generally one-tenth the muscle size of men who worked in the same weight program. The reason is that most women do not produce male hormones in sufficient quantity to develop large muscles.

Results of recent international competitions show that countries that encourage women to use weights develop better athletes. The best example is the performance by the East German women's swimming team at the 1976 Montreal Olympics. The East German women won 11 out of 13 gold medals. The secret to their success, according to their coach, was a comprehensive weight-lifting program. It has been estimated that 40 per cent of the swimmers on the American women's Olympic team, which won only one gold medal in Montreal, had never lifted weights. "Most [American women] swimmers," gold-medalist Shirley Babaschoff said, "are afraid of getting too big."[8]

The Status of Women in Professional Sports

There are at present no women competing in the Big Four professional sports leagues—Major League Baseball, the National Basketball Association, the National Hockey League and the National Football League. Player salaries in those leagues have climbed steeply in recent years. The average salary for Major League Baseball players in this year's opening-day lineups was some $95,000. It is estimated that the average NBA player's salary is $109,000.[9]

[7] Quoted in *The National Observer*, July 31, 1976.

[8] Quoted by Diana Nyad, "Pumping Iron," *womenSports*, April 1977, p. 48. See also Cheryl McCall, "Who's Afraid of Bulging Biceps? A Call to Arms for Women Athletes," *Ms.*, May 1977, p. 26.

[9] Figures compiled in a United Press International survey, published in *The Washington Post*, April 10, 1977.

One way to measure differences in opportunities for women and men in professional sports is to compare monetary compensation and the amount of television time given to males and females in golf and tennis—the only pro sports in which women's earnings even remotely compare to men's. There had never been more than two women's professional golf tournaments on national television until this year. Seven Ladies Professional Golf Association (LPGA) tournaments will be televised in 1977. Overall, the women will be competing for $3.2-million in prize money. The total prize money on the male Professional Golfers Association tour is some $9-million. LPGA officials say that the difference in prize money is directly related to television exposure. Until this year, PGA tournaments were televised nearly every weekend during the spring and early summer, leaving women golfers with much less desirable mid-week dates for their tournaments.

While women such as Chris Evert and Billie Jean King have won fame and large incomes in professional tennis, male pro tennis stars average nearly double the women's earnings. The United States Tennis Association's list of money winners through Dec. 9, 1976, showed the top male winner, Jimmy Connors, with $687,335. The leading woman, Chris Evert, earned $343,165. The No. 2 money winners were Ilie Nastase ($479,205) and Evonne Goolagong ($209,952). At last year's prestigious All-England (Wimbledon) tennis tournament, Evert, the women's division winner, won $17,700, while Bjorn Borg, the men's champion, took home $22,500. Evert and the other women players have asked that the prize money be the same for both sexes. Evert said, "I'm absolutely determined not to defend my title next year unless the women get equal parity."[10] A survey of all professional sports showed that "in nine out of 10 cases, the men's prize money figures are higher than the women's in the same sport."[11]

Women did make some advances in motorized racing last year. Janet Guthrie was the first woman to file for entry in the Indianapolis 500 race. Shirley Muldowny won the National Hot Rod Association World Final race, driving a 1,500-horsepower dragster 249.30 miles per hour—the second fastest recorded time in that category. Kitty O'Neil, who has been a champion swimmer, diver, water skier, motorcycle racer and Hollywood stunt woman, came close to breaking the world land speed record when she drove a three-wheeled rocket car 612 miles per hour on the Alvord Desert in Oregon.

Women have been professional jockeys since the late 1960s.

---

[10] Quoted in *womenSports*, September 1976, p. 50.
[11] Ellen Weber, "The Pros Lag Behind," *womenSports*, September 1974, p. 35.

And there are professional opportunities for women in bowling, basketball, soccer, volleyball and even football. But those professional sports offer women little national exposure and they cannot hope to reap the large incomes enjoyed by their male counterparts.

Title IX's Impact on Athletics

A MERICAN WOMEN have been discouraged from partici- pating in competitive sports since they were organized in the 19th century. Some colleges developed sports and athletic programs for women in the 1920s. But the inclusion of sports as a regular part of women's college educations was short-lived. A reaction against girls' basketball by those who thought women in short pants should not perform before male crowds created an anti-sports climate for women by the 1930s. "When I went to college in the Thirties, we were taught that competition was dir- ty," Betty Desch, head of women's physical education at a New York college, has said.[12] Girls' sports programs were eliminated at many colleges. Women's teams were reduced to the "club" level and intercollegiate competition was cut sharply.

The attitudes of the 1930s hampered the athletic develop- ment of women in this country for decades. For years, budgets for sports activities in elementary and secondary schools and es- pecially in colleges and universities were weighted heavily in favor of males. It is generally agreed that until a few years ago fiscal outlays for women's sports in the nation's colleges were only 1 per cent of men's totals.

Things began to change in the late 1960s, pushed by the women's liberation movement and by state and national civil rights legislation. The laws[13] led to a series of court rulings banning discrimination against women in nearly every branch of sports competition, from Little League baseball to collegiate sports. By far the most important regulation affecting women and sports is Title IX of the Education Amendments of 1972, which prohibits sex discrimination in any activity sponsored by a school receiving federal funds.

Title IX regulations, which apply to some 16,000 school dis- tricts and 2,700 colleges and universities, stipulate that schools

[12] Quoted by Bil Gilbert and Nancy Williamson, "Sport is Unfair to Women," *Sports Illustrated,* May 28, 1973, p. 93.
[13] In addition to Title IX of the Education Amendments of 1972, laws affecting women's sports include Title VII of the 1964 Civil Rights Act, which prohibits all employers with more than 14 employees from discriminating against employees on the basis of sex, race, religion or national origin; The Equal Protection Clause of the Fourteenth Amendment to the U.S. Constitution; and Equal Rights Amendments passed in many states.

sponsoring interscholastic, intercollegiate or intramural sports must provide equal athletic opportunities for members of both sexes. These schools are required to establish women's teams in sports for which men's teams exist. If there is not enough interest to make up a separate women's team, women must be allowed to try out for the men's team if the sport does not involve bodily contact. Schools may allow women to try out for men's contact sports, such as football and basketball, but are not required to do so. Separate teams for contact sports must be formed if enough women want them. Schools that do not comply with Title IX face the loss of federal aid, a threat that has been termed the "first significant pressure on most local school districts to change their interscholastic sport program policies."[14]

NCAA's Reaction to Title IX Requirements

Many college coaches, athletic directors and officials of the National Collegiate Athletic Association (NCAA)—the governing body of men's intercollegiate sports—reacted angrily to the new regulations. The NCAA said that Title IX supporters saw the rules "as a means of dismantling intercollegiate athletics."[15] The rules, the NCAA added, "may well signal the end of intercollegiate athletic programs as we have known them in recent decades." The new rules do not require schools to spend equal amounts of money on women's and men's sports. But they do call for equal treatment for male and female athletes in terms of equipment, scheduling of games and practice times, travel and daily expenses, coaching, lodging, training and playing facilities, publicity and athletic scholarships.

The NCAA and other athletic groups lobbied intensely to have the Title IX rules overturned by Congress.[16] Their efforts were successfully opposed by a variety of women's groups, including the Women's Equity Action League and the Association for Intercollegiate Athletics for Women, and some educators' groups. But some women's organizations, including the National Organization for Women's Project on Equal Education Rights, argued that the Title IX rules would perpetuate many forms of discrimination rather than eradicate them. They said that some of the regulations were so vaguely worded as to leave the rules open to varying interpretations and eventual litigation.

The deadline for elementary schools to comply with the Title IX regulations was July 21, 1976. Nine months later, it still is

---

[14] Janice Pottker and Andrew Fishel, "Separate and Unequal: Sex Discrimination in Interscholastic Sports," *Integrated Education,* March-April 1976.

[15] Editorial in the *NCAA News,* July 15, 1975. For a further discussion of college athletics, see "Future of Varsity Sports," *E.R.R.,* 1975 Vol. II, pp. 645-664.

[16] The NCAA spent "more than $200,000 lobbying to avoid sharing a dime with women," according to Candace Lyle Hogan in *womenSports,* February 1976, p. 45.

Who's Who in Women's Sports Movement

American Alliance for Health, Physical Education and Recreation (AAHPER)—parent group of seven organizations, including associations of teachers, coaches and administrators in physical education. Affiliated with the National Education Association.

Association for Intercollegiate Athletics for Women (AIAW)—governing body of women's intercollegiate sports. AIAW represented some 787 members during the 1976-77 school year and is affiliated with AAHPER.

Center for Women and Sports—founded at Pennsylvania State University in 1973 to expand research on the female athlete.

National Association for Girls and Women in Sports (NAGWS)—membership includes women coaches and physical education teachers. Affiliated with AAHPER, NAGWS seeks to increase sports opportunities for women.

National Organization for Women Task Force on Sports—works for equal rights for women in school athletics, public recreation, legislation, media coverage.

Project on Equal Education Rights (PEER)—an affiliate of the National Organization of Women's Legal Defense Fund. Monitors Title IX enforcement, including sex discrimination in sports.

Project on the Status of Education of Women—affiliated with the Association of American Colleges. Monitors federal enforcement of laws prohibiting discrimination by sex in elementary and secondary schools.

Resource Center on Sex Roles in Education—maintains a clearinghouse on sex role stereotyping in education, including sex discrimination in sports. Affiliated with the National Foundation For the Improvement of Education.

Women's Equity Action League (WEAL)—involved in assisting Title IX enforcement on all levels. Provides a "sports kit" that focuses on the inequities in athletics and on the Title IX regulations.

Women's Sports Foundation—involved in several projects to promote women in sports, including the development of a Women's Hall of Fame.

not known exactly how many schools have complied with the rules. A survey taken last fall in the Washington, D.C., area found that "in general, all area school systems report that their elementary-school physical education classes have been, or will be this year, coed as required by HEW regulations."[17] The sur-

[17] *The Washington Post*, Oct. 29, 1976.

vey also showed that "a large majority" of the Washington, D.C., area's intermediate and senior high school physical education classes were coed, even though the deadline for secondary schools is not until July 21, 1978. Most of those polled said they believed that the Title IX regulations were responsible for the changes in elementary and secondary schools.

Closely tied to changes in athletic programs are the fiscal problems facing school districts across the country. *The Wall Street Journal* reported late last year that because of funding shortages and inflation "school officials increasingly are regarding sports as the fat man in the crowded educational lifeboat."[18] Large cities have been affected the hardest. The Detroit school board was forced to stop all interscholastic sports and some other activities when a tax levy was voted down last August. Only a $146,000 contribution from a bank saved some of the varsity sports. Without additional funding, the entire interscholastic athletic program in Detroit will be terminated next fall.

Donations from corporations and individuals were needed to maintain high school football competition in St. Louis in 1975. In Buffalo, N.Y., a private fund drive last year collected some $67,000 to support boys' football and cross-country, and girls' volleyball. New York City was not so fortunate. Two years ago, all junior-varsity teams in the city's 100 public high schools were eliminated when the school board budget was cut by 40 per cent. All intramural programs were dropped last year. Although the problem is most pronounced in large cities, smaller jurisdictions also face similar fiscal problems.

In spite of the cutbacks and financial pressures, there is evidence that overall interscholastic sports participation has increased during the last four years, especially among girls. The National Federation of State High School Associations, whose membership includes the 50 state high school athletic associations, said that in the 1972-1973 school year, 800,000 girls and 3.8 million boys took part in high school sports in this country. For the 1975-1976 school year, the latest year for which figures are available, the federation reported the boys' total to be some 4 million and the girls' total 1.3 million.

Interscholastic basketball is the most popular girls' sport in the United States. Some 14,427 high schools fielded teams and 380,000 girls participated in 1975-1976, according to the National Federation of State High School Associations' Sports Participation Survey. Interest in this sport continues to pick up all over the country. Record crowds have been reported; 5,100 persons attended a first-round game in the 1977 Kentucky state

---

[18] *The Wall Street Journal,* Nov. 3, 1976.

girls' basketball tournament in March. The Wisconsin state girls' basketball tournament, in its second year, increased the 1976 attendance some 30 per cent—45,000 to 58,000. In contrast, attendance at the boys' regional and sectional tournament dropped to 289,502, down from the 1976 total of 298,259. Matt Otte, associate director of the Wisconsin Interscholastic Athletic Association, commented: "What's happening is that the girls' crowds, especially in the smaller towns, are cutting into the boys' crowds."[19]

No discussion of girls' high school basketball would be complete without mention of the program in Iowa, where girls' basketball is more popular than boys'. This year, Southeast Polk High School in Des Moines won the girls' state championship March 12 before a crowd of 14,512 in Des Moines' Veterans Memorial Auditorium. One reason for the popularity of girls' basketball in Iowa is that equal opportunities exist for both sexes in everything from coaching to media coverage and awards banquets. Kim Peters of Andrew (Iowa) High School was named to an all-America high school girls' basketball team this year by *Parade* magazine.[20] It was the magazine's first all-star list in girls' basketball, after two decades of selecting outstanding boys in the sport.

Continued Unequal Treatment at Colleges

There is little doubt that women's athletics have been underfinanced at a majority of colleges and universities. According to an American Council of Education study completed in 1974, most college athletic budgets allotted women only 0.5 per cent to 3 per cent as much as men.[21] Women's athletics' budgets have risen since that time. But they still lag far behind.

Last year, for example, the University of Florida granted 38 women's athletic scholarships on a budget of some $140,000. The men's budget at Florida covered 216 scholarships and was some $3.5-million. There are plans to award 88 scholarships to women and increase the women's athletic budget to $200,000. But Athletic Director Ray Graves has said: "I don't know if the women's budget will ever be comparable. There's just so much [revenue] you can get out of football. We're approaching that limit now. There's just no way you can hire a full-time coach for, say [women's] gymnastics."[22]

At the University of Minnesota, the 1976 women's athletic budget of some $330,000 funded 10 different sports. The budget

---

[19] Quoted in *The Wisconsin State Journal*, March 20, 1977.

[20] April 10, 1977, issue.

[21] Mary McKeown, "Women in Intercollegiate Athletics," Appendix H of "An Inquiry into the Need for Feasibility of a National Study of Intercollegiate Athletics," report to the American Council of Education, March 22, 1974.

[22] Quoted in the *St. Petersburg Times*, May 27, 1976.

for Minnesota's 11 men's varsity teams was $2.9-million. The University of Texas' athletic budget for women increased from $27,500 in 1974 to $128,000 in 1976. But the scope of women's athletics at Texas is dwarfed by the men's. There are 21 full-time coaches for men and seven part-time coaches for women; 216 athletic scholarships for men and only 10 for women. At the University of Maryland, the athletic department budget of $2.28-million allocated $227,816 to women's sports in 1976.

Yale University's sports budget for men is some $1.7-million annually. The women's sports program receives only $300,000 even though one-third of Yale's undergraduates are women. Fifteen women athletes and women's tennis coach Judith Dixon have filed a complaint with the Department of Health, Education and Welfare in an effort to have Yale's sports budget distributed more equally. In addition, Dixon has resigned as coach and assistant to the director of athletics for sports information. She has filed suit in U.S. District Court in New Haven, Conn., charging that the university practices sex discrimination. It is believed that Dixon's suit is the first of its kind in a federal court.

In June 1976, *womenSports* magazine conducted a random survey of 55 colleges and universities to determine the effect of Title IX on women's sports. By comparing facilities, equipment, practice schedules, jobs and salaries, the magazine concluded that "by and large women have more support in school sports now than they ever had, but clearly college women athletes are not being treated as well as men." The "most definitive thing that can be said about the status of women in college athletics" since the passage of Title IX "is that while before they had nothing, now they have something."[23]

The Chronicle of Higher Education contacted a number of faculty members and administrators at colleges and universities involved with implementing Title IX last year. It reported that, in general, colleges and universities "have been slow to change their discriminatory policies because the costs are too high. What's more...judging by past actions, it will be years before the federal government begins to enforce Title IX seriously, if it ever does."[24] Some large state universities reported that it will be very difficult for them to provide equal opportunities for women by July 21, 1978, the HEW deadline.

Many state universities have asked state legislatures for extra funds to finance women's sports, but they have few expectations of getting additional money from the financially

---

[23] Candace Lyle Hogan, "Fair Shake or Shakedown?" *womenSports*, September 1976, p. 50.

[24] Anne C. Roark, "Federal Sex-Bias Forms Seen Inviting Dishonesty," *The Chronicle of Higher Education*, Dec. 6, 1976, p. 8.

strapped state treasuries. Most small colleges have had comparatively few problems complying with the Title IX regulations. Schools without large-budget men's sports programs generally are able to grant more women's scholarships and provide equal facilities. But some small, private colleges say that fiscal problems prevent them from hiring more women's coaches or equalizing salaries.

Prospects for Change in Future

T WO ISSUES are central to the future of women in sports: exactly how women's intercollegiate sports will be administered and what body will have authority over them. The governing body for women's intercollegiate sports is the Association of Intercollegiate Athletics for Women (AIAW), which was formed in 1971 and is recognized by 787 schools. The National Collegiate Athletic Association (NCAA), founded in 1905, administers the men's sports programs at 707 colleges and universities. The NCAA has been challenging the AIAW for control of women's college sports for several years.

An overriding question in the NCAA-AIAW dispute is whether the administration of women's intercollegiate sports ultimately will be based on the male NCAA model, a highly competitive program that has become a multi-million-dollar business at many universities. As more colleges enlarge budgets for women's sports and award more women's scholarships—especially in basketball—pressure to recruit top high school athletes is increasing. Abuses in recruiting and subsidizing athletes have been one of the NCAA's biggest problems since athletic scholarships and grants-in-aid were first given to men in the 1890s.

Until the spring of 1973, the AIAW did not allow women on athletic scholarships to participate in AIAW-sanctioned events. That action, which amounted to a ban on athletic scholarships for women, reflected the thinking of a large group of women in athletics who believed that recruiting and awarding of scholarships led to serious problems. "When the AIAW was formed, many men told us that scholarships were a bad influence on collegiate sports," Mary Rekstad, a former AIAW executive, has said. "They said we should avoid making the mistakes they had made and stay out of the mess."[25]

Four years ago the AIAW membership voted to allow women to accept scholarships. But the association has retained other rules designed to avoid recruiting excesses. For example,

---

[25] Gilbert and Williamson, *op. cit.*, p. 92.

expense-paid visits by high school athletes to college campuses are not allowed. The rules also forbid payment to coaches to travel around the country to recruit high school athletes. At the Fourth Annual AIAW Delegate Assembly last January the membership voted, 206-145, to continue the ban on paying coaches to recruit. At the meeting, the association also voted to limit athletic scholarships to tuition and fees only, starting in August 1978.

Popularity of Women's Basketball in College

Basketball is the fastest-growing women's sport on college campuses across the nation. Some observers fear that if the sport continues its rapid growth, it will soon face the recruiting problems that men's college sports contend with. The number of scholarships for women has risen rapidly since 1973, the first year the AIAW permitted them. Late last year, *The New York Times* estimated that some 5,000 to 8,000 female athletic scholarships were available nationwide, many of them to basketball players.[26]

The University of California at Los Angeles is one of many large schools that have begun to upgrade women's basketball. UCLA has granted scholarships to nearly all of its 15 varsity players and it actively recruits talented high school players. "We know we have to recruit and we do," UCLA Women's Athletic Director Judith Holland said recently. "But we'd never 'buy' kids, as I've heard they do at other schools. I'm not saying we'll always be pure—money distorts the picture. But recruiting doesn't have to be vicious. We'll never hound kids."[27] UCLA reportedly has considered soliciting alumni contributions to set up a recruiting fund; the AIAW does not allow the financing of coaches' recruiting trips from women's athletic budgets.

UCLA's program is just getting started on a large scale. So far two small schools have dominated women's intercollegiate basketball—they have won all six AIAW national championships. The winner of the first three national titles, Immaculata College, has 500 students and is located in suburban Philadelphia. Delta State College of Cleveland, Miss., which defeated the University of Tennessee, 62-58, on March 26, 1977, to take its third straight AIAW basketball title, has 3,200 students.

Some 640 colleges competed in 1976-77 compared with 215 schools five years earlier. One sportswriter has written that the game "has jumped light years in image, talent and draw. The giggles and cynics have been silenced. The barriers have

[26] *The New York Times,* Nov. 14, 1976.
[27] Quoted by Ted Green, "Basketball Goes Big-Time at UCLA," *womenSports,* March 1977, p. 27.

crumbled." [28] The first all-women's basketball doubleheader at a major American sports arena was held on March 6, 1977, in New York City's Madison Square Garden—a traditional showcase for men's basketball. A crowd of 12,336 watched four of the nation's top teams, including Delta State and Immaculata.

One reason for the increased popularity of the women's game is that the level of play has risen greatly. Delta State's Lucy Harris, a star on the U.S. women's team that placed second in the 1976 Olympics, is "the first dominant big woman in college basketball."[29] Among the many other talented players are Ann Meyers of UCLA, a member of the 1976 Olympic team and the first woman at UCLA to receive a full athletic scholarship; Carol Blazejowski of Montclair (N.J.) State College, who scored 52 points, a Madison Square Garden record, in the March 6 game; and Nancy Dunkle of California State University at Fullerton, a three-time all-American and member of the Olympic team.

The Struggle For Control of College Sports

The rise of women's collegiate basketball portends many things. There is little doubt that many colleges are attracting larger crowds for games. The revenue from paid admissions and radio and television broadcast rights could make women's basketball a revenue-producing sport at many colleges. It has been alleged that the possible financial success of women's college basketball is the primary reason the NCAA wants to control women's intercollegiate sports.

A motion was considered at the 1975 NCAA convention on what role the organization should assume in the governance of women's intercollegiate sports. The measure never came to a vote, and the question was assigned to a committee for study. Meanwhile, the NCAA and AIAW formed a joint committee to discuss the matter.

In 1976, Cal Papatsos of Queens College, New York, Katherine Ley of Cortland College, New York, and Celeste Ulrich of the University of North Carolina at Greensboro became the first women to participate as delegates in an NCAA convention. All three opposed NCAA control of women's sports. Without debate, a proposal that the association establish women's championships in a number of sports was sent back to committee. At the 1977 NCAA convention in Miami Beach, the women's sports issue did not come up. In the summer of 1976, the NCAA withdrew from the joint NCAA-AIAW committee and formed its own standing panel to deal with women's athletics. The new committee had only one woman member and no AIAW representative.

---

[28] Seymour S. Smith in *The Baltimore Sun*, March 15, 1977.
[29] Bil Gilbert, "The Smaller Stood Taller," *Sports Illustrated*, April 4, 1977, p. 59.

What concerns some women sports administrators above all is a suit filed in 1975 against HEW by the NCAA, challenging HEW's interpretation of the Title IX sports regulations. Pretrial motions were heard April 11 in U.S. District Court in Kansas City, Kan., before Judge Earl O'Connor. Lawyers for AIAW joined with HEW attorneys to argue against the NCAA claim that Title IX is illegal because some programs covered by the sports regulations do not receive federal funds. NCAA officials maintain that the suit is not a challenge to the AIAW's control of women's intercollegiate sports. They say that the suit is intended only to determine the scope of Title IX. "We are trying to find out what Title IX really means," Tom Hansen, an NCAA assistant executive director, has said.[30]

Future Role of Women in the Sports Arena

The NCAA and the AIAW are not the only organizations concerned with Title IX. A section on women and sports was included in the Final Report of the President's Commission on Olympic Sports, issued Jan. 13, 1977. The commission, set up in 1975 to study amateur athletics in the United States, cited the medical, moral and social myths that have kept women from gaining equal opportunities in sports. The report endorsed Title IX and recommended that a body be established to govern all amateur sports in this country and that it "give priority to the many issues concerning women's role in athletics." The report recommended the development of "methods to ensure that women play an equitable role in all aspects of sports with reasonable opportunities for participation."[31]

President Carter himself has expressed support for Title IX. In answer to a questionnaire from *Women Today* magazine, Carter said last year, "I do not approve of excepting physical education from the Title IX regulations of the Education Amendments of 1972.... I have always felt that physical health is vital to mental health, and excluding women from equal opportunities to participate in all types of sports would be unfair. I would like to see my daughter Amy be able to excel in any sport she might choose, just as my sons have been able to do. I would oppose any legislation that would weaken the provisions of Title IX."[32]

The American Council of Education last year set up a commission to undertake a three-year study on the problems of intercollegiate sports. Among the issues the commission will examine are the extent of discrimination against women as participants, coaches and administrators; how colleges can comply

---

[30] Quoted in *The Washington Post*, Jan. 16, 1976.
[31] "The Final Report of the President's Commission on Olympic Sports," January 1977, p. 110.
[32] *Women Today*, March 15, 1976.

Women Sportswriters

Women sportswriters once were rarities on American newspapers. There were few female applicants for sportswriting jobs, for one thing. And those women who tried to cover sports were barred by long-standing tradition from entering men's locker rooms and press boxes at most sports arenas. But things are changing. The movement for women's equality in athletics has helped spawn a marked increase in the number of female sportswriters across the country. Many big-city newspapers have at least one woman sportswriter.

One of the best known is Lynn Rosellini of *The Washington Star.* Two years ago Rosellini wrote a widely acclaimed series on homosexuals in sports—a subject largely ignored by male sportswriters. Other women sportswriters, such as Nancy Scannell of *The Washington Post,* specialize in economic, social and psychological issues. Scannell's beat deals mainly with player strikes, lawsuits and federal legislation affecting sports. Other women report on all aspects of sports, including day-to-day coverage of men's college and professional sports. Some specialize in women's sports.

One woman sportswriter who is not a newcomer is Mary Garber of the *Winston-Salem Journal.* Garber began covering sports in 1944 when she moved from editing the society page to the sports desk due to a wartime shortage of male sports reporters. She has remained on the sports beat ever since.

with Title IX; and whether sports should be conducted on a sexually integrated or separate-but-equal basis. The commission, which has been funded by a $200,000 grant from the Ford Foundation, includes several college presidents. It also will examine several of the current problems facing the NCAA, including recruiting ethics.

It is evident that women's athletics have progressed significantly in the last few years. But there still are many inequities. Men's sports continue to get by far the biggest share of attention in the media, as a glance at any sports page will show. Colleges and universities continue to fund men's sports generously and women's sports far less generously. And professional sports opportunities for women lag significantly behind those for men. Opportunities on all levels have increased, though, and clearly the trend is for further advances.

Some women are worried about the direction the women's sports movement is taking. They question the advisability of molding women's collegiate athletics on the male model, which places heavy emphasis on winning and has evolved into a semi-professional, high-pressure enterprise. But some female athletes fear that if they deviate from the male model, no one will take them seriously.

Selected Bibliography

Books

Gerber, Ellen W., et. al., *The American Woman in Sport,* Addison-Wesley, 1974.

Haney, Lynn, *The Lady is a Jock,* Dodd Mead, 1973.

Michener, James A., *Sports in America,* Random House, 1976.

Novak, Michael, *The Joy of Sports,* Basic Books, 1976.

The Boston Women's Health Book Collective, *Our Bodies, Ourselves,* Simon and Schuster, 1973.

Articles

"About Women's Athletics," *NCAA News,* July 15, 1975.

Dunkle, Margaret, "College Athletics: Tug-of-War for the Purse Strings," *Ms.,* September 1974.

La Noue, George R., "Athletics and Equality," *Change,* November 1976.

McCall, Cheryl, "Who's Afraid of Bulging Biceps? A Call to Arms for Women Athletes," *Ms.,* May 1977.

Pottker, Janice and Andrew Fishel, "Separate and Unequal: Sex Discrimination in Interscholastic Sports," *Integrated Education,* March-April 1976.

Sports Illustrated, selected issues.

The Chronicle of Higher Education, selected issues.

womenSports, selected issues.

Reports and Studies

Boring, Phyllis Z., "A Feminist Looks at Sports," Women's Equity Action League, 1977.

Dunkle, Margaret C., and Bernice Sandler, "Sex Discrimination Against Students: Implications of Title IX of the Education Amendments of 1972," Project on the Status and Education of Women, Association of American Colleges, November 1975.

Dunkle, Margaret C., "Title IX: What it Means and Doesn't Mean to Athletic Programs," Project on the Status and Education of Women, Association of American Colleges, Nov. 11, 1976.

—"What Constitutes Equality for Women in Sport?" Project on the Status and Education of Women, Association of American Colleges, September 1975.

Editorial Research Reports, "Future of Varsity Sports," 1975 Vol. II, p. 645; "Women's Consciousness Raising," 1973 Vol. II, p. 497.

National Foundation for the Improvement of Education, Resource Center on Sex Roles in Education, "Competitive Athletics: In Search of Equal Opportunity."

President's Commission on Olympic Sports, "Final Report," January 1977.

U.S. Department of Health, Education and Welfare, Office of Civil Rights, "Final Title IX Regulation Implementing Education Amendments of 1972," June 1975.

—"Memorandum to Chief State School Officers, Superintendents of Local Educational Agencies and College and University Presidents, Subject: Elimination of Sex Discrimination in Athletic Programs," September 1975.

ABORTION POLITICS

by

Sandra Stencel

Oct. 22
1 9 7 6

ABORTION POLITICS

O NE OF THE major surprises of the 1976 election campaign has been the prominence of the abortion issue. From the opening days of the presidential primary season last January, both political parties and their candidates have been under heavy pressure from dedicated groups and individuals demanding endorsement of strong stands favoring or opposing legalized abortion. Since the formal start of the general election campaign on Labor Day, President Ford and his Democratic opponent, Jimmy Carter, continually have been asked to define and redefine their stands on this emotion-laden, divisive and complex question.

Most of the impetus has come from groups working to overturn a Supreme Court decision upholding a woman's constitutional right to choose to have an abortion. The court ruled, on Jan. 22, 1973, that only during the final three months of pregnancy can the state constitutionally prohibit abortions *(see p. 112)*. The court later extended women's abortion rights by ruling, July 1, 1976, that a woman need not obtain spousal or parental consent to have an abortion.[1]

Since it was legalized in 1973, abortion has become the most frequently performed surgical procedure in the nation. Nearly one million legal abortions were performed in the United States in 1975, according to a recent study by the Alan Guttmacher Institute,[2] based on statistics gathered by the U.S. Department of Health, Education and Welfare.[3]

That means that more than one-fifth of all pregnancies last year were terminated by abortion. Approximately 300,000 abortions for women on welfare were financed by the federal government at a cost of $45-million, primarily under Medicaid programs for the poor. The question of whether federal funds should continue to be used to pay for abortions for low-income women has become an election issue. A new law forbids federal

---

[1] *Planned Parenthood of Central Missouri v. Danforth,* 44 U.S.L.W. 5197.

[2] See Edward Weinstock, *et al.,* "Abortion Needs and Services in the United States, 1974-75," *Family Planning Perspectives,* March-April 1976, p. 58. *Family Planning Perspectives* is published by the Planned Parenthood Federation of America under the direction of its research and development division, the Alan Guttmacher Institute.

[3] HEW's figures on abortion were: 742,460 in 1973; 899,850 in 1974; and 998,020 projected for 1975.

aid for abortions except when the woman's life is endangered. However, the law has been challenged in federal court and its effective date, Oct. 1, delayed by temporary restraining orders. Opponents of the measure acted in an effort to prevent the Department of Health, Education and Welfare from ending Medicaid payments for abortions until the law's constitutionality is decided.

Positions Taken by Candidates Ford and Carter

Ford and Carter have gone on record opposing federal payments for abortions. Both candidates have said that they oppose abortion on demand and favor abortion only in specific cases, including pregnancies that endanger the life of the mother or result from rape or incest. The President's position differs from Carter's on the question of a constitutional amendment to reverse the Supreme Court's 1973 ruling. The President has said that while he disagrees with the court's decision, he opposes a constitutional amendment to ban abortions nationwide. Rather, he favors a constitutional amendment which would permit each state to draw up its own abortion law. Carter, on the other hand, has said that he opposes either type of constitutional amendment.

Ford, in a White House press conference Sept. 8, said that he was more than willing to have abortion become an issue in the presidential campaign. "I don't think the American people expect candidates for office to duck any issues just because they are intense, with good people on both sides having different views," he said. "I think the American people ought to get an answer from Governor Carter and myself on this issue just like on any other issue." Carter, in a speech the following day in Columbus, Ohio, agreed with the President that abortion was a "legitimate" campaign issue and one that he, as a candidate, took seriously.

Both Ford and Carter have been accused of "flip-flopping" on the abortion issue. The President's declared opposition to an outright constitutional ban on abortions is said by some political observers to conflict with his stated support for the Republican platform plank on abortion. It states that the party "supports the efforts of those who seek enactment of a constitutional amendment to restore protection of the right to life for unborn children." This has been interpreted in some quarters as calling for a constitutional amendment to prohibit abortion in most cases.

Carter appeared to soften his opposition to a constitutional amendment after he met with six Roman Catholic bishops in Washington on Aug. 31. Archbishop Joseph Bernardin of Cincinnati, chairman of the National Conference of Catholic

Bishops—a leading force in the anti-abortion move-ment—reported that Carter told the bishops he would not oppose others who were seeking a constitutional amendment. Carter later explained that he had taken this position because he did not like the wording of the Democratic platform plank. It states: "[I]t is undesirable to amend the U.S. Constitution to overturn the Supreme Court decision in this area." Carter said the wording implies a moral judgment of those who do seek an amendment, a judgment he does not wish to make. But Carter's opponents pointed out that his chief issues adviser, Stuart Eizen-stat, helped write the abortion plank and lobbied for it.

Reasons for Abortion's Rise to Prominence

The visibility of abortion as a campaign issue is surprising because public opinion polls have consistently indicated that only a minority of voters consider a candidate's position on abortion to be a major factor in their voting decisions. Analyzing the results of a national poll taken by *The New York Times* and CBS News in early September, political reporter R. W. Apple Jr. found abortion to be a "clearly non-partisan" issue. "The voters' position on...abortion was unrelated either to their Ford-Carter choice or to their party preference," he wrote.[4]

A recent Mervin D. Field poll of California voters showed that only 25 per cent of the people questioned thought abortion was a "very important" consideration when choosing a President; 44 per cent said that it was not important.[5] A national poll com-missioned by the National Conference of Catholic Bishops, released in March 1975, showed that slightly more than 44 per cent of the 4,067 persons polled—Catholics and non-Catholics—said that abortion was not sufficiently important to them to be the sole issue on which to base their vote. Thirteen per cent agreed with the statement "stopping abortion is so im-portant that I would vote against any candidate who supports abortion, no matter how many things we agreed on," while 15 per cent took the position that "the right to abortion is so impor-tant that I would vote against any candidate who opposed abor-tion, no matter how many things we agreed on."

The question therefore arises: Why has abortion become one of the most visible and volatile issues of the presidential cam-paign? According to Robert Teeter, director of research for the Ford campaign committee, abortion is "symbolic" of a whole range of issues and views on which a large portion of the American people cast their ballot. These voters, he said, "are conservative in life-style rather than in an ideological sense...and they are afraid of radical social patterns."[6]

---

[4] *The New York Times*, Sept. 10, 1976.
[5] Reported in the *Los Angeles Times*, Sept. 19, 1976.
[6] Quoted in *The New York Times*, Sept. 21, 1976.

The Edelin Conviction

An offshoot of the anti-abortion movement was conviction of a Boston gynecologist, Dr. Kenneth Edelin, in connection with a legal abortion he performed in October 1973 on a 17-year-old woman in her 22nd to 24th week of pregnancy. He was charged with having killed the fetus by withholding air from the womb for three minutes. A Boston jury, on Feb. 15, 1975, found Dr. Edelin guilty of manslaughter. Although the charge carried a maximum penalty of 20 years in prison, a Massachusetts state court judge gave the doctor a one-year suspended sentence and placed him on probation. The verdict has been appealed.

The legality of the abortion was not challenged. At issue was the question of when does a fetus become a person, a question the U.S. Supreme Court left unanswered in its 1973 ruling *(see p. 112)*. The prosecution in the Edelin case charged that the aborted fetus had been capable of surviving outside the womb and, therefore, the doctor had an obligation to try to keep the fetus alive. By failing to do so, the prosecution maintained, Edelin had caused the baby's death and was guilty of manslaughter.

To assess the impact of the Edelin conviction on the medical community, *McCall's* magazine (June 1975) polled a nationwide sampling of obstetrician-gynecologists. The survey indicated that 42 per cent were much warier than before about performing abortions, particularly those taking place after the first 12 weeks of pregnancy.

Another view was offered by N. Robert Heyer, editor of the Field poll. "All political candidates are understandably nervous about an issue such as this, which touches people's personal lives, and which does not follow the line of standard political party issues," he said. "The danger to a candidate of an issue like this is that it may drive away some of the supporters who could normally be expected to support him on other issues, without attracting a like number from the other side."[7]

Religious Divisions Over 'Pro-Life' Advocacy

Many observers attribute the prominence of the abortion issue to the zeal, passion and organization of those strongly opposed to legalized abortion. Single-minded, angry and persistent, the "right-to-life" minority makes itself seen and heard. In the forefront of political action against abortion is the National Right to Life Committee, a non-sectarian group with headquarters in Washington. The committee claims to represent more than a million members and it has an annual budget of $300,000. None of the budget comes from the Catholic Church, according to the committee's former executive director, Ray L. White.

---

[7] Quoted in the *Los Angeles Times*, Sept. 19, 1976.

The Catholic Church has been active in the anti-abortion movement from the start. But this year it is more visible than ever before and much more involved in direct confrontations with politicians over the question of a constitutional amendment. The basic argument of the Catholic hierarchy is that the fetus is a person from the moment of conception, and, as such, has a right to be protected from "murder." Similar stands have been taken by the Eastern Orthodox Churches, the Lutheran Church-Missouri Synod, the Church of Jesus Christ of Latter-day Saints (Mormons), and some small fundamentalist denominations.

But the religious community, like the rest of society, is divided on the abortion issue. Many Protestant and Jewish organizations in the United States support legalized abortion. Some see attempts to overturn the Supreme Court's ruling as a threat to the constitutional rights of women and to freedom of religion. In August 1973 a group of Protestant and Jewish leaders established a coalition to coordinate religious efforts to protect the legal option of abortion. Called the Religious Coalition for Abortion Rights, it currently has 24 member groups.[8]

To counter the political activities of the "right-to-life" movement, the coalition and the National Abortion Rights Action League on Sept. 28 announced the opening of an "11th hour" drive to elect pro-abortion candidates in November to preserve access to "safe and legal" abortions. Karen Mulhauser, executive director of the Abortion Rights League, charged that "right-to-life" groups and the American Catholic hierarchy had elevated abortion to a "hot political issue" when it should be a "private" one. John D. Rockefeller III, chairman of the Population Council, shares this view:

> Abortion is against the moral principles defended by the Roman Catholic Church, and some non-Catholics share this viewpoint. But abortion is not against the principles of most other religious groups. Those opposed to abortion seek to ban it for everyone in society. Their position is thus coercive in that it would restrict the religious freedom of others and their right to make a free moral choice.[9]

---

[8] National Ministries, American Baptist Churches; American Ethical Union; American Jewish Congress, Women's Division; National Women's Conference of the American Ethical Union; American Humanist Association; B'nai B'rith Women; Catholics for a Free Choice; Division of Homeland Ministries, Disciples of Christ; National Council of Jewish Women; National Federation of Temple Sisterhoods; General Executive Board, Presbyterian Church in the U.S.; Union of American Hebrew Congregations; Unitarian Universalist Association; Unitarian Universalist Women's Federation; Board of Homeland Ministries, United Church of Christ; Center for Social Action, United Church of Christ; Board of Church and Society, United Methodist Church; Women's Division, Board of Global Ministries, United Methodist Church; Church and Society Unit, United Presbyterian Church, USA; Women's Program Unit, United Presbyterian Church, USA; Women's League for Conservative Judaism; Young Women's Christian Association; Committee on Women's Concerns, Presbyterian Church in the U.S.; Washington Office, United Presbyterian Church, U.S.A.

[9] John D. Rockefeller III, "No Retreat on Abortion," *Newsweek*, June 21, 1976, p. 11.

The anti-abortion forces have had little success in mustering congressional support for placing a proposed constitutional amendment before the states for approval. The Senate Judiciary Subcommittee on Constitutional Amendments, on Sept. 17, 1975, after 18 months of hearings, rejected all proposed anti-abortion amendments. The House Judiciary Subcommittee on Civil and Constitutional Rights held hearings on the abortion question in February and March 1976, but did not act on the proposed amendments. Sen. Jesse A. Helms (R N.C.), in an effort to bring the abortion issue to the full Senate for a vote before the 1976 election, used a parliamentary maneuver to bypass committee action on a proposed constitutional amendment to guarantee unborn children the right to life. The Senate, showing no wish to take up the issue in an election year, voted, 47 to 40, to table it—in effect killing it.

Efforts of Catholic Hierarchy to Ban Abortion

Frustrated by the lack of action in Congress, the "pro-life" movement turned its attention to the 1976 election. A "Pastoral Plan for Pro-Life Activities," adopted by the National Conference of Catholic Bishops at its annual meeting in Washington in November 1975, called for formation of interdenominational "pro-life" groups in all 435 congressional districts to influence the 1976 campaign. These groups should work "to convince all elected officials and potential candidates that the 'abortion issue' will not go away...."

The impact of the abortion issue was demonstrated in the Jan. 19 Iowa precinct caucuses—the first test of voter attitudes in the 1976 campaign. A few days before the caucuses, Carter was quoted in *The Catholic Mirror,* the Des Moines diocesan newspaper, as saying that he supported "a national statute which would restrict the practice of abortion." This was interpreted by many to mean Carter favored a constitutional amendment prohibiting abortions. Carter won the backing of Iowa's Catholic hierarchy and went on to win the caucus vote. His victory in Iowa won him the label of Democratic frontrunner. But Carter later explained he did not mean that he supported a constitutional amendment.

While the abortion issue came to public view in the Iowa caucuses, it was the New Hampshire primary on Feb. 24 that first focused the news media's attention on Ellen McCormack, a Catholic housewife who had entered the Democratic presidential primaries on a "pro-life" platform. Although few political observers considered Mrs. McCormack a serious candidate, her campaign drew publicity to the anti-abortion cause and forced the other candidates to take a stand on the issue. She campaigned in 17 state primaries, and at the Democratic National Convention she received 22 delegate votes.[10]

However, her presence did not prevent the adoption of an abortion plank that would outrage the Catholic hierarchy and other "pro-life" groups. Archbishop Bernardin labeled the Democrats' position as "irresponsible" and "morally offensive," and he urged Catholics to generate opposition to it. The opposition increased after the Republicans adopted their anti-abortion plank. Hoping to mollify Catholic leaders, Carter met with Archbishop Bernardin and five other bishops on Aug. 31. The bishops said afterward they were "disappointed" by Carter's continued opposition to a constituional amendment. After a similar meeting with President Ford on Sept. 10, the bishops said they were "encouraged" by the President's support for a constitutional amendment to let the states regulate abortions.

The bishops' statements were generally interpreted as an endorsement of Ford over Carter. This drew criticism as well as praise from other Catholics. The executive board of the National Federation of Priests' Councils said the hierarchy's preoccupation with abortion obscured other important issues.[11] The liberal Catholic journal *Commonweal* warned the bishops that their confrontation with Carter over abortion "could result in a significant backlash against them and the entire Catholic community."[12]

Responding to such criticism, Archbishop Bernardin announced at a news conference in Washington on Sept. 16 that the hierarchy had not endorsed either candidate and would not do so. However, Cardinal Cooke told worshipers at St. Patrick's Cathedral in New York 10 days later that while the Catholic Church would not endorse either candidate, it "cannot be neutral" on abortion. This theme was echoed in thousands of parishes across the country on Oct. 3, the date of this year's "Respect Life Sunday," sponsored annually by the bishops' committee for pro-life activities.

Assessing the Catholic Vote and Its Importance

American Catholics appear divided on the abortion question, according to public opinion polling,[13] despite the strong stand

---

[10] Much of the publicity centered on whether a single-issue candidate should be entitled to taxpayer support. The 1974 Federal Election Campaign Act provided for public financing of presidential elections, and McCormack qualified for over $250,000 in federal matching funds. This led Congress to amend the 1974 act. Under the revised law, signed by President Ford on May 11, 1976, presidential candidates who receive less than 10 per cent of the vote in two successive primaries will, in 30 days, become ineligible for further matching funds.

[11] Letter to Terence Cardinal Cooke of New York, who heads the bishops' pro-life committee.

[12] "Carter and the Bishops," *Commonweal*, Sept. 24, 1976, p. 613.

[13] A Gallup Poll released in June 1975 showed that 50 per cent of the Catholic respondents would sanction abortion under some circumstances; an additional 17 per cent thought abortion should be legal in all circumstances; and only 32 per cent said abortion should be illegal in all circumstances.

taken by their leaders. Nonetheless, neither Ford nor Carter can afford to ignore the potential effect of abortion on even a minority of the 33 million voting-age Catholics. This is especially true of Carter since Catholics traditionally have been an important Democratic constituency. In five of the last six elections, a majority of Catholics voted Democratic.[14] But when the Catholic vote for the Democratic candidate fell below 60 per cent, as it did in 1972, 1968, 1956 and 1952, the Democrats lost.

The Christian Science Monitor reported Sept. 9 that Carter's support among Catholics was running about 54 per cent. But a national poll taken for NBC News in mid-September found Carter with only a one percentage point lead over Ford (44 to 43) among registered Catholic voters. Carter's relative weakness among Catholic voters goes beyond his stand on abortion. Some Catholics link the Southern Baptist candidate to the tradition of southern fundamentalism, which was often strongly anti-Catholic.[15] In addition, a large proportion of Catholic voters of ethnic origins are troubled by Carter's relatively liberal image, according to political scientist Seymour Martin Lipset of Stanford University[16]

While Ford and Carter vie for the Catholic vote, they face the possibility of a backlash vote by the advocates of legalized abortion. After Carter's meeting with the Catholic bishops, the National Women's Political Caucus accused him of "a betrayal of the Democratic platform." "The result of your waffling on this issue," they said, "will be to alienate women who want to know where you stand." Ford was accused by the Women's Political Caucus of making "cynical and ill-advised" use of the abortion controversy as a campaign issue.

Abortion Reform Movement, 1959-73

T HE CURRENT abortion controversy was triggered by the Supreme Court's ruling in 1973 that the abortion laws of Texas and Georgia violated the right to privacy guaranteed by the U.S. Constitution.[17] The court's decisions were the final stages of litigation in two separate cases: *Roe v. Wade* (Texas) and *Doe v. Bolton* (Georgia). The names Roe and Doe were the pseudonyms of two women who had sued public officials for denying them the right to have safe legal abortions.

[14] The exception was in 1972, when Richard Nixon won 52 per cent of the Catholic vote against George McGovern's 48 per cent.

[15] See "Politics and Religion," *E.R.R.*, 1976 Vol. II, p. 621.

[16] Seymour Martin Lipset, "The Catholic Defection," *The New Republic*, Oct. 2, 1976, p. 11.

[17] See Harriet F. Pilpel, Ruth Jane Zuckerman and Elizabeth Ogg, "Abortion: Public Issue, Private Decision," *Public Affairs Pamphlet No. 527*, September 1975.

The Texas case challenged the state's criminal statutes that outlawed all abortions except those performed to save the life of the woman. After reviewing much of the medical, social, religious, historical and legal material relating to abortion, the Supreme Court concluded that the right of privacy, "founded in the Fourteenth Amendment's concept of personal liberty...is broad enough to encompass a woman's decision whether or not to terminate her pregnancy." However, the court said that the right to an abortion was not absolute. At certain times a state's interest in preserving the health of the mother or the potential life of the unborn infant becomes sufficient to justify some degree of regulation of abortion.

The Supreme Court decided that during a woman's first three months of pregnancy, the state could not place any restrictions on her decision to procure an abortion except to require that it be performed by a physician. In the second three months of pregnancy, the state's duty to protect its citizens entitles it to specify conditions under which an abortion may be performed. A state could, for example, stipulate that abortion facilities meet certain standards, and that after-care services and means of dealing with possible complications be provided. However, during this stage the state could not limit the reasons for which women may have abortions. Only during the final trimester of pregnancy, when the fetus is judged to be capable of surviving outside the mother's womb, may the state, if it chooses, ban abortions other than those performed to save the life of the mother.

In *Roe v. Wade,* the Supreme Court considered the question: When does life begin? The "pro-life" movement contends that life begins at the moment of conception. The court recognized "the vigorous opposing views" among physicians, theologians, philosophers and others as to when life begins and concluded that it could not resolve this "difficult question."

Justice Harry A. Blackmun, writing for the majority,[18] said: "When those trained in the respective disciplines of medicine, philosophy and theology are unable to arrive at any consensus, the judiciary, at this point in the development of man's knowledge, is not in a position to speculate as to the answer." However, the majority opinion concluded that legally the word "person" as used in the Constitution applies only after birth and that, therefore, the Fourteenth Amendment's provision that no person shall be deprived of "life, liberty, or property, without due process of law" does not apply to the unborn.

---

[18] The majority was composed of Blackmun, Chief Justice Warren E. Burger, Associate Justices Lewis F. Powell Jr., William O. Douglas, Potter Stewart, Thurgood Marshall and William J. Brennan Jr. Justices Byron White and William H. Rehnquist dissented.

But while the fetus is not a "person" with constitutional rights, the court said that once viability is reached, that is, once the fetus was capable "of meaningful life outside the mother's womb," the state has sufficient interest in the potential life of the fetus to be allowed to intervene in abortions.

The Georgia abortion law, also struck down, was relatively more liberal. It permitted abortion (1) to protect the life or health of the pregnant woman, (2) in cases of rape, and (3) if the fetus was likely to be born with "a grave, permanent, and irremediable mental or physical defect." Applying the principles set forth in the Texas case, the court found the Georgia limitations unconstitutional. It devoted much attention to Georgia restrictions on women's access to abortion. It struck down requirements that an abortion be performed (1) only in accredited hospitals, (2) only after approval by the hospital's abortion review committee and agreement by three doctors that the abortion should be performed, and (3) only on legal residents of the state.

The abortion decisions were both lauded and condemned. Patrick Cardinal O'Boyle of Washington, D.C., called them "a catastrophe for America" and Cardinal Cooke said they were "shocking and horrifying." In contrast, the Rev. Dr. Howard E. Spragg, executive vice president of the Board of Homeland Ministries of the United Church of Christ, said: "The decision is historic not only in terms of women's individual rights, but also in terms of the relationships of church and state."

Earlier Liberalization in Courts and Legislatures

The Supreme Court's pronouncement climaxed a 14-year struggle to liberalize abortion laws in the United States.[19] That struggle had begun, very tentatively, with the Model Penal Code proposed by the American Law Institute in 1959. The code included a provision that a licensed physician could legally terminate a pregnancy if he or she believed that: (1) it threatened the life or would gravely impair the physical or mental health of the mother; (2) the child would be born with a grave physical or mental defect; or (3) the pregnancy resulted from rape or incest. The code also required two physicians, one of whom might be the doctor who would do the abortion, to file certificates with the hospital where the operation would be performed, stating their belief in the justifying circumstances.

The thalidomide tragedy of 1962 triggered a serious movement for abortion reform. In that year, many babies—primarily in West Germany—were born grossly deformed because, during pregnancy, their mothers had taken an insufficiently tested drug called thalidomide. Pregnant women who had taken the

---

[19] See "Abortion Law Reform," *E.R.R.*, 1970 Vol. II, pp. 543-562.

Public Hospitals Providing Abortion Services

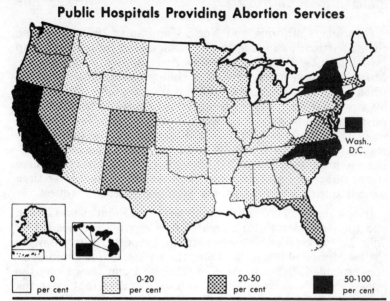

| | 0 per cent | | 0-20 per cent | | 20-50 per cent | | 50-100 per cent |

Source: The Alan Guttmacher Institute, based on 1974 and early 1975 statistics.

drug and feared they would give birth to deformed infants desperately sought abortions. One, Sherri Finkbine of Phoenix, Ariz., had arranged for a therapeutic (and therefore legal) abortion, prescribed by her doctor and approved by the local hospital board. But because her life was not in immediate danger, the county prosecutor threatened legal action and the hospital withdrew its sanction. Mrs. Finkbine then obtained an abortion in Sweden. The fetus was seriously deformed.

A rubella epidemic occurred in the United States in 1964. By that time the danger of German measles to a fetus in early stages of pregnancy was widely understood, and some women demanded and obtained legal abortions. But large numbers found legal restrictions and lack of money to be insurmountable barriers; they either ran the risk of delivering defective infants or had illegal abortions.

The thalidomide and rubella cases helped create a climate in which abortion reform could move forward. Two other developments of the 1960s contributed to the growing abortion-law reform movement, according to Jimmye Kimmey, executive director of the Association for the Study of Abortion. "One was the civil rights movement, which highlighted those individual rights that no state could abridge. (To many people, abortion was one of those rights.) The other was the growing honesty and openness about human sexuality. This made it easier to discuss abortion in public as well as in private."[20]

[20] Jimmye Kimmey, "How Abortion Laws Happened," *Ms.*, April 1973, p. 118.

Colorado, California and North Carolina in 1967 liberalized their abortion laws along the lines suggested by the American Law Institute. By 1973, 13 states had adopted such statutes. Much more sweeping legislative changes came about in 1970 when Alaska, Hawaii, New York and Washington State (the last by a popular referendum) legalized all abortions performed by physicians up to a fixed time in pregnancy. The New York law was the most liberal of the four. It permitted abortion for any reason up to the 24th week of pregnancy; after that, only abortions to preserve a mother's life were permitted. The other three states imposed state residency requirements and shorter time periods during which abortions were permitted on request.

In the spring of 1972, the Commission on Population Growth and the American Future, created by Congress and headed by John D. Rockefeller III, issued its final report. After reviewing the restrictive abortion laws and their effects, the commission recommended "liberalization of state abortion laws along the lines of the New York State statute." Earlier that year the American Bar Association had approved a Uniform Abortion Act as a model for all states. It was drafted by the Conference of Commissioners on Uniform State Laws and was based largely on the 1970 New York law.

While state legislatures were beginning to reexamine their abortion laws, state and lower federal courts were being asked to rule on their constitutionality. In 1969, in *People v. Belous,* the California Supreme Court held unconstitutional an old state law banning all abortions except those necessary to save a woman's life.[21] After that, a number of other state and federal courts declared similar laws void because of vagueness or for interfering with a woman's right to privacy. Not only were several of the most restrictive laws declared unconstitutional but so, too, were some of the newer, more liberal laws, mainly because of the limitations they placed on the grounds for abortion.[22]

Post-1973 State Laws; Effect on Public Health

The Supreme Court's 1973 decision forced repeal or revision of criminal abortion statutes in every state—including those that had liberalized their abortion laws along the lines of the American Law Institute's model. At least 34 states[23] enacted new abortion laws. Some of the new laws were consistent with the Supreme Court's ruling. But others attempted to qualify or limit women's access to abortion by requiring such things as parental or spousal consent. Most of these restrictions have been

---

[21] California had enacted a less-restrictive statute in 1967, but the abortion in this case had been performed earlier.

[22] See Lawrence Lader, *Abortion II: Making the Revolution* (1973), pp. 186-195.

[23] Ariz., Ark., Calif., Ga., Idaho, Ill., Ind., Ky., La., Maine, Md., Mass., Mich., Minn., Miss., Mo., Mont., Neb., Nev., N.J., N.Y., N.C., N.D., Ohio, Pa., R.I., S.C., S.D., Tenn., Utah, Vt., Va., Wis. and Wyo.

found unconstitutional, first by lower courts and subsequently by the Supreme Court.

Perhaps the single most important result of the Supreme Court's decision was to reduce the risks of medical complications and death associated with illegal abortions. The National Academy of Sciences issued a study, "Legalized Abortion and the Public Health," in May 1975, which documented the sharp decline in the number of deaths related to abortion after the 1973 decision. According to the report: "Risks of maternal death associated with legal abortion are low—1.7 deaths per 100,000 first trimester procedures in 1972 and 1973—and less than the risks associated with illegal abortion, full-term pregnancy, and most surgical procedures. The 1973 mortality rate for a full-term pregnancy was 14 deaths per 100,-000 live vaginal births...." The report also said: "While abortion may elicit feelings of guilt, regret or loss in some women, these reactions tend to be temporary and appear to be outweighed by positive life changes and feelings of relief."

Quest for Constitutional Restriction on Abortion

Proposals to overturn the Supreme Court ruling by constitutional amendment were introduced in Congress immediately after the decision. In general, the amendments fell into two categories—"right-to-life" amendments and "states' rights" amendments. The first type would overturn the Supreme Court ruling that the fetus is not a person with constitutional rights. It would guarantee rights to life to the unborn at "every stage of their biological development" or "from the moment of conception." Some "right-to-life" amendments proposed to ban abortions in any circumstances; others, such as the one introduced by Sen. James L. Buckley (Cons R N.Y.), sought to permit abortions in "an emergency when a reasonable medical certainty exists that continuation of the pregnancy will cause the death of the mother." The second type of constitutional amendment would return to the states the right to decide whether and when abortions would be legal.

Before any of the anti-abortion amendments can be adopted, one of two routes must be followed. One requires passage of the amendment by a two-thirds vote in both houses of Congress, followed by ratification by two-thirds of the states. The second route requires the calling of a constitutional convention upon the request of two-thirds of the states. The amendment would then require approval by a majority at the convention and ratification by three-fourths of the states.

The U.S. Commission on Civil Rights delivered a blow to the "pro-life" movement on April 14, 1975, when it issued a report strongly opposing any of the proposed constitutional amendments. The commission concluded that "so long as the question of when life begins is a matter of religious controversy and no choice can be rationalized on a purely secular premise, the people, by outlawing abortion through the amendment process, would be establishing one religious view and thus inhibiting the free exercise of religion of others."[24]

Issues for Post-Election Period

A BORTION is sure to remain a divisive issue long after the November election. The "pro-life" movement has pledged to continue the campaign for an anti-abortion amendment to the Constitution. Amendment proposals are expected to reappear in the 95th Congress, which comes into session in January 1977.

Public opinion polls indicate that public sentiment for legalized abortion is growing. The people who responded to a Gallup Poll in March 1974 were almost evenly divided on the question—47 per cent for and 44 per cent opposed. A nationwide survey conducted by *The New York Times* and CBS News in February 1976 showed that 67 per cent of the respondents agreed with the statement: "the right of a woman to have an abortion should be left entirely up to the woman and her doctor." The Knight-Ridder newspapers asked a similar question in a survey they took a month earlier and found 81 per cent in agreement. In March, a survey sponsored by *The National Observer* found 71.4 per cent in favor of letting the Supreme Court decision stand.

Groups in favor of legalized abortion are less concerned about the possibility of a constitutional amendment than about continued efforts in Congress to attach anti-abortion riders to bills dealing with other matters. Four such riders have been adopted since 1973:

> An amendment to the 1973 Foreign Assistance Act prohibits the use of foreign aid funds for abortions "as a method of family planning."

> An amendment to the Legal Services Act of 1974 forbids legal services' attorneys from helping low-income women secure "nontherapeutic" abortions.

> An amendment to the Health Programs Extension Act of 1973 provides that a hospital's receipt of federal funds does not require

[24] United States Commission on Civil Rights, "Constitutional Aspects of the Right to Limit Childbearing," April 1975, p. 31.

it "to make its facilities available for the performance" of abortions or sterilizations "if the performance of such procedures" violates "religious beliefs or moral convictions."

An amendment to the 1977 appropriations bill for the Departments of Labor and of Health, Education and Welfare bans the use of federal funds to pay for abortions "except where the life of the mother would be endangered if the fetus were carried to term."

Planned Parenthood, the National Abortion Rights Action League, the American Civil Liberties Union and other groups in favor of legalized abortion are fighting to block implementation of the latest abortion restriction. Anti-abortion forces had lobbied for a ban on Medicaid payments for abortions for over three years. An opponent of the measure, Jeannie I. Rosoff, director of the Washington office of Planned Parenthood, accused Congress of "collapsing under election-year pressure."[25]

Those who opposed the Medicaid ban argued that it was unconstitutional because it discriminated against the poor. *The Washington Post* commented editorially on Sept. 17 that it was "a rich women's amendment, one leaving abortion available to those who can afford to have it performed." *The New York Times* said in an editorial the same day that the law would establish "the principle of two-class medicine." *Ms.* magazine declared: "Denial of Medicaid reimbursement for abortion makes no sense if 'equal protection under the law' is to extend beyond the middle class."[26]

Abortion Decisions Before the Supreme Court

Supporters of the amendment deny these charges. "The fact that a woman has a qualified right to an abortion does not imply a correlated constitutional right to free treatment," said U.S. Solicitor General Robert H. Bork in a friend-of-the-court brief submitted on behalf of the government in cases due to be considered by the Supreme Court in its 1976-77 term. The cases challenge laws in Pennsylvania and Connecticut that prohibit the use of public funds for abortions except in instances where the mother's life is endangered.

In the Pennsylvania case, *Beal v. Doe,* the U.S. Court of Appeals for the Third Circuit (Philadelphia) ruled in 1975 that Pennsylvania's refusal to pay for non-therapeutic abortions violated Title XIX of the 1965 Social Security Act, which set up the Medicaid program. The appeals court said that once a state agrees to pay for maternity care for poor women, or for therapeutic abortions, it must also pay for elective abortions. In

---

[25] *Planned Parenthood Washington Memo,* Sept. 16, 1976.
[26] Denise Spalding, "Abortions: Legal But How Available?" *Ms.*, September 1975, p. 103.

the Connecticut case, *Maher v. Roe,* a three-judge federal district court held that the state's refusal to pay for non-
therapeutic abortions for the poor violated the equal-protection
clause of the Constitution.[27]

If the Supreme Court upholds the ruling that the denial of
Medicaid funds for abortions violates the Fourteenth
Amendment's equal-protection clause, the anti-abortion provision of the Labor-Health, Education and Welfare
appropriations bill would be nullified. Federal funds would have
to be used for abortions unless a constitutional amendment was
adopted to cut off the federal financing of abortions. On the
other hand, if the Supreme Court rules that the states' denial of
funds for abortions violates the law setting up the Medicaid
program, Congress could pass a new law specifically prohibiting
the use of Medicaid funds for abortions.

The Supreme Court also has agreed to review an April 1975
ruling *(Poelker v. Doe)* by the U.S. Court of Appeals for the
Eighth Circuit (St. Louis) that the city of St. Louis acted un-
constitutionally in banning abortions at municipally operated
hospitals and in staffing those hospitals solely with personnel
opposed to abortion on religious grounds. The appeals court said
this policy infringed on a pregnant woman's right to privacy and
denied low-income women equal protection under the law.

Concern over Distribution of Abortion Services

Although nearly one million abortions were performed
nationwide in 1975, at least 260,000 and perhaps as many as
770,000 women who needed an abortion were unable to obtain
one, according to the Alan Guttmacher Institute. Most of these
women were poor or lived in rural areas. Abortion services tend
to be distributed unevenly *(see map)* among and within the
states. Generally they are concentrated in one or two
metropolitan areas where most abortions are performed in non-
hospital clinics. According to the institute's study, more than
half of the abortions in early 1975 were performed in clinics.
Only about one-fourth of the non-Catholic, general hospitals in
the United States—about one-third of the privately administered hospitals and fewer than one-fifth of the public
hospitals—reported performing even a single abortion in 1974
and early 1975, the period covered by the institute's study.

There were 10 states in which no public hospitals reported
performing even one abortion in 1974 and early 1975. In 14 other
states fewer than one in 10 public hospitals reported providing
any abortions. In only nine states and the District of Columbia

---

[27] The Fourteenth Amendment states that no citizen shall be denied "the equal protection of the laws."

did at least half of all non-Catholic general hospitals—public and private—report they performed any abortion in 1974 and early 1975. Only four states and the District of Columbia reported that half or more of their public hospitals provided abortion services.

"Unless hospitals—especially public hospitals—initiate legal abortion services on a broader scale than at present," the Institute's report concluded, "it seems likely that in numerous states and localities, poor, rural and teenage women—who are least able to travel to obtain legal abortions—will continue to be unable to obtain the services they want and need." Increasing the availability of abortion services is just one goal of the "pro-choice" movement. An equal concern is improving the quality of existing abortion services. In some places women's groups have begun monitoring abortion facilities, working for lower costs and for adequate counseling. Worried that abortion clinics were becoming too commercialized and profit-oriented, feminist groups have begun setting up their own women-run, non-profit abortion clinics.

Many people feel that the best way to deal with the abortion controversy is to reduce the need for abortions to the absolute minimum. But until family planning methods and services are perfected, made universally available and totally safe, there will be women who suffer unwanted or accidental pregnancies. If past history is any guide, many of them will choose to have abortions—legal or not.

Selected Bibliography

Books

Callahan, Daniel, *Abortion: Law, Choice and Morality*, Macmillan, 1970.

Hardin, Garrett, *Mandatory Motherhood: The True Meaning of Right to Life*, Beacon Press, 1974.

Lader, Lawrence, *Abortion II: Making the Revolution*, Beacon Press, 1973.

Sarvis, Betty and Hyman Rodman, *The Abortion Controversy*, Columbia University Press, 1973.

Articles

Alpern, David, "Courting the Catholics," *Newsweek*, Sept. 20, 1976.

Commonweal, selected issues.

Lader, Lawrence, "Abortions Denied," *The Nation*, July 17, 1976.

Kimmey, Jimmye, "How Abortion Laws Happened," *Ms.*, April 1973.

Lipset, Seymour Martin, "The Catholic Defection," *The New Republic*, Oct. 2, 1976.

Loomis, David, "Abortion: Should Constitution Be Amended?" *Congressional Quarterly Weekly Report*, May 3, 1975.

Ms., selected issues.

Otten, Vicki, "New Attack on Abortion Rights," *Americans for Democratic Action Legislative Newsletter*, Aug. 1, 1976.

Sauer, R., "Attitudes To Abortion in America, 1800-1973," *Population Studies*, March 1974.

The Human Life Review, fall 1976 issue.

Weinstock, Edward, *et al.*, "Abortion Need and Services in the United States, 1974-1975," *Family Planning Perspectives*, March-April 1976.

"Ban All Abortions?" *U.S. News & World Report*, Sept. 27, 1976.

"On Abortion, the Bishops v. the Deacon," *Time*, Sept. 20, 1976.

Reports and Studies

Editorial Research Reports, "Abortion Law Reform," 1970 Vol. II, p. 543; "Contraceptives and Society," 1972 Vol. I, p. 415.

Institute of Medicine, "Legalized Abortion and the Public Health," National Academy of Sciences, May 1975.

Pilpel, Harriet F., Ruth Jane Zuckerman and Elizabeth Ogg, "Abortion: Public Issue, Private Decision," *Public Affairs Pamphlet No. 527*, September 1975.

U.S. Commission on Civil Rights, "Constitutional Aspects of the Right to Limit Childbearing," April 1975.

INTERNATIONAL WOMEN'S YEAR

by

Suzanne de Lesseps

June 13
1 9 7 5

INTERNATIONAL WOMEN'S YEAR

THE CONDITION of women around the world is under scrutiny this year. The United Nations has declared 1975 International Women's Year, and the women's movement hopes that more than mere lip service will be paid to upgrading the status of women throughout the world. "We have it in our power to make this Year a truly valuable and important advance in the position of women in the social, economic, cultural and political process," said U.N. Secretary-General Kurt Waldheim in December 1974, "or, alternatively, merely to make it a ceremonial occasion devoid of practical meaning."[1]

The United Nations is highlighting the year by sponsoring a world conference on women June 19-July 2, 1975, in Mexico City. It will be the first major inter-governmental meeting ever held that is devoted to the status of women in society. Participating nations will discuss the current roles of women and their involvement in national and international affairs. The delegates will be called on to approve a "World Plan of Action," outlining objectives and goals for improving the position of women over the next 10 years.

Women are still subject to various forms of discrimination, whether overt or subtle, in nearly every country. Though women make up about half of the world's population,[2] they are vastly underrepresented in public life almost everywhere. Some of the most obvious forms of discrimination can be attributed to religious law and custom. In Saudi Arabia, for example, the religious police have the power to spray women's legs with black paint if they appear in public without the traditional dress. Dr. Promilla Kapur, a specialist in the sociology of women, has written that in a number of Hindu households in India, the birth of a daughter is cause for sorrow, while the birth of a son is cause for much attention and celebration.[3]

The marriage laws in several countries deprive women of personal rights as well as property rights. In many cases the husband is recognized as the head of the family, and the wife is

---

[1] Quoted in the *U.N. Monthly Chronicle*, January 1975, p. 64.
[2] 49.8 per cent, according to United Nations figures.
[3] Promilla Kapur, "Myth or Reality?" *World Health* (publication of the U.N. World Health Organization), January 1975, pp. 8-11.

given little legal voice in family decisions. In Mexico, the Philippines and Uruguay, for example, she must get special permission from her husband to exercise such legal rights as signing a contract or bringing a law suit. In some other countries, she must obtain his authorization to engage in trade or industry.

According to the United Nations, nine countries still do not give women full political rights.[4] Yet even in countries where they have been accorded political rights for many years, women are not as active as men in public affairs and government. According to Helvi Sipila, U.N. Secretary-General for International Women's Year, "too few women in either the developed or the developing countries participate in formulating and implementing national, regional, or international policies relating to development and population."[5]

Economic Issues and Family Planning Programs

The relationship between the status of women and population-control programs was defined in a study prepared by Ms. Sipila and presented to the U.N. Commission on the Status of Women in January 1974. The study [6] emphasized several conclusions, including the following:

> When women recognize the benefits of family planning, they will be free to seek roles other than motherhood. Alternative roles must be available for women to assume.

> Fertility is more affected by the educational level of the wife than by the educational level of the husband.

> High fertility goes hand in hand with the low status of women. Family planning programs cannot succeed without improvements in the condition of women.

> High fertility patterns are both the result and cause of underdevelopment, thus setting a vicious cycle in motion.

The participants at the U.N. International Forum on the Role of Women in Population and Development, held in New York in February 1974, also spoke of a "vicious cycle" created by overpopulation and the low educational and employment status of women. "The disadvantages women suffer are likely to be exacerbated by population pressures and trends which place a severe strain on available resources," Margaret K. Bruce, deputy director of the U.N. Centre for Social Development and Humanitarian Affairs, said at the conference. "For women usually lose out if they must compete with men for limited educational facilities and limited job opportunities."[7]

---

[4] Bahrain, Kuwait, Liechtenstein, Nigeria (in six states), Oman, Qatar, Saudi Arabia, United Arab Emirates and Yemen.

[5] "Women and World Affairs," by Helvi Sipila, *Today's Education*, November-December 1974, p. 67.

[6] U.N. Economic and Social Council, Report of the Special Rapporteur, "Study on the Interrelationship of the Status of Women and Family Planning," Nov. 27, 1973.

[7] U.N. Document OPI/CESI NOTE IWY/1, April 1974.

Prominent International Women

Indira Gandhi
Prime Minister of India

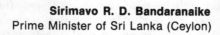
Sirimavo R. D. Bandaranaike
Prime Minister of Sri Lanka (Ceylon)

Margaret Thatcher
Leader of the Conservative Party in Britain

Simone de Beauvoir
author of *The Second Sex*

Betty Friedan
founding member of the National Organization for Women.

Helvi Sipila
U.N. Secretary-General for International Women's Year and Assistant Secretary-General for Social Development and Humanitarian Affairs

At the U.N.-sponsored World Population Conference in Bucharest, Rumania, in August 1974, female participants strongly insisted that women be given a larger voice in efforts to solve the problems of overpopulation. "I don't want to hear anymore a man say what a woman from the Third World wants or doesn't want," said Dr. Dora Obi Chizea of Nigeria, interrupting a session of the conference.[8]

The World Plan of Action approved by the population conference in Bucharest recognized that the improved position of women in society was a necessary factor in lowering fertility rates. As a result of lobbying from a group of women, including Margaret Mead, Betty Friedan and Germaine Greer, the plan acknowledged the right of women to contribute to economic development and other activities on an equal basis with men. Helvi Sipila regarded almost all of the recommendations adopted by the conference as related in some way to upgrading the status of women.

Women are also heavily involved in the international problem of food shortages. As much as 50 per cent of the food in the developing countries is produced by women; in Africa, they comprise 60 to 80 per cent of the agricultural labor force. "...The introduction of agricultural technology and mechanization has not involved women," stated a Food and Agriculture Organization background paper written for the International Women's Year conference in Mexico City, "nor has it decreased their work schedules."[9] Recognizing the role of women in food production, the U.N.-sponsored World Food Conference in Rome in November 1974 adopted six resolutions containing specific references to women's rights and their role in economic development. One resolution was devoted entirely to women and food.

Importance of Women in the World Labor Force

"Women's role in rural development needs to be more fully explored," stated a recent report of the International Labor Organization (ILO) titled *Equality of Opportunity and Treatment for Women Workers* (1975). "If productivity in rural areas is to rise, they [women], as essential family providers need to know about agricultural power, rural crafts, animal husbandry, food processing and marketing." The ILO report projected that developing regions would account for 70 per cent of the world's female labor force by the year 2000.

Prepared as the basis for a discussion on equal treatment for women workers at the International Labor Conference in

---

[8] Quoted in *The Washington Post*, Aug. 27, 1974.
[9] U.N. World Conference of the International Women's Year, *The Role of Women in Rural Development*, Document E/Conf. 66/BP/11, March 24, 1975, p. 15.

Geneva in June 1975, the ILO study is a compendium of statistics on the status of female workers around the world. On the basis of census results available up to 1971, the ILO estimates that in 1975 women account for about 34 per cent of the world's 1.6 billion paid laborers, in figures shown below:

Area	Females in Labor Force	Area	Females in Labor Force
Africa	30.9%	South Asia	29.7%
Latin America	19.6	Europe	34.4
Northern America	35.0	Russia	49.3
East Asia	38.9	Oceania	30.4

The ILO report emphasized that women are still underpaid. Comparisons between the wage earnings of men and women in manufacturing—often the only sector for which statistics are available—pointed out that women's wages were about 50 to 80 per cent of those received by men. But women's wages have been increasing at a faster rate than those of men *(see box, p. 139)*. Despite the prevailing prejudices against women in employment, the ILO stated, there has been substantial improvement in the status of working women in many parts of the world. The report mentioned Britain, France, Spain, Scandinavia, Japan, the Arab states, the United States and Australia as countries that have worked toward ending discrimination against female workers.[10]

Origins of the Feminist Movement

CURRENT BELIEFS in male dominance and superiority can be traced to the beginnings of patriarchal society. The term "patriarchy" has ancient roots, going back at least to biblical times.[11] The word describes a household in which father is the supreme head. All wives and children are legally dependent upon him, and all rights are passed down through male descendents. In true patriarchal families, women are prohibited from owning property.

Patriarchal supremacy was diffused somewhat in ancient Babylonia. Women were granted a fair amount of legal and economic freedom, and women of the upper classes were allowed

[10] The Commission of the European Communities, executive agency for the European Economic Community (Common Market), approved in February 1975 a draft directive calling for equal treatment for men and women in all areas of employment.
[11] See "The Persistence of Patriarchal Thinking" by Lynne B. Iglitzin in *The Center Magazine*, May-June 1974.

full property rights. Quite the opposite was true in ancient Greece, where women were not permitted to work outside the home, and young women were granted only maintenance and dowry rights. The Greek philosopher Plato, however, was a strong defender of female equality and even admitted a few women to his academy. In *The Republic*, Plato argued that "since they are competent and of a like nature" as men, women should share equally in all rights and public duties.[12] Plato's pupil, Aristotle, disagreed with his mentor on this point and believed that women were inferior and should be ruled by men.

In early Roman times, a woman was under the sole domination of her husband. Gradually, however, this changed. She began to retain close ties with her father and as a result did not become a legal member of her husband's family. She was able to acquire her own property rights, had a greater choice in whom she married, and had equal divorce rights with her husband. The great amount of legal and social freedom enjoyed by Roman women was later denounced by early Christian leaders who saw it as a sign of moral decay. "As Christianity became dominant throughout Europe," wrote Bernhard J. Stern in the *Encyclopaedia of the Social Sciences*, "women were deprived of that freedom which they had attained in Rome...."[13] In the view of the Church, women were basically dependent and subordinate.

Emergence of Feminism in Nineteenth Century

In western medieval society, demographer Philippe Ariés argued in his book *Centuries of Childhood* (1962), the family was loosely organized and made few demands on its members. Since little attention was paid to offspring, women had considerable freedom and some were allowed to work in crafts and trades. The primary function of the family unit was to carry on the name and property rights. During the 16th century, however, the family became more private. Children were given more attention, particularly in education, and as a consequence, women took on more reponsibilities. Domestic life became more and more demanding until, in the 19th century, women's energies were concentrated in the home. Historian William L. O'Neill said Ariés' thesis enabled him to understand why women suddenly became tired of family burdens in the 19th century and why they sought to free themselves.[14]

Other reasons are also offered for the emergence of feminism in England and America during the 19th century. The coming of

---

[12] *The Republic of Plato*, translated with introduction and notes by Francis M. Cornford, p. 153.

[13] "Women: Historical Position in Society," *Encyclopaedia of the Social Sciences* (1939), Vol. VIII, p. 444.

[14] William L. O'Neill, *The Woman Movement: Feminism in the United States and England* (1969), p. 17.

the industrial revolution opened up more job opportunities for women, freeing them from the domestic confines of the household and enabling them to meet new friends. Women also gained more say in family matters since they were now contributing to the family as wage earners.

One ramification of industrialization was an increase in the importance of the working class. Democratic demands for more personal freedom became frequent, and in some ways women's rights became caught up in the general cause. The influence of Enlightenment thinking also contributed to a new revolutionary spirit. An early 18th century philosopher, Condorcet, spoke out in favor of female emancipation, and in 1789 Olympe de Gouges wrote a feminist tract titled *The Declaration of the Rights of Women.*

Mary Wollstonecraft's *A Vindication of the Rights of Women*, published in England in 1792, was heavily influenced by the French Revolution. But French revolutionary leaders had not been totally sympathetic to feminist causes. In 1789 they refused to accept a Declaration of the Rights of Women when it was presented at the National Assembly. One of the philosophical founders of the revolution, Jean Jacques Rousseau, had written in 1762:

> The whole education of women ought to be relative to men. To please them, to be useful to them, to make themselves loved and honored by them, to educate them when young, to care for them when grown, to counsel them, to make life sweet and agreeable to them—these are the duties of women at all times, and what should be taught them from their infancy.[15]

The rise of liberalism is also often cited as a reason for the rise of feminism during the 19th century. The British reform movement of the 1830s sought to improve the working conditions of women through legislation. The Mines Act, for instance, prohibited women from working underground. During debate on the Reform Bill of 1867, John Stuart Mill introduced an unsuccessful amendment calling for female enfranchisement. Mill also helped to found the first women's suffrage society, later known as the National Union of Women's Suffrage Societies. In 1869 he published *The Subjection of Women*—the classic argument for women's suffrage which served as the basic text for women's movements around the world. His thesis was:

> That the principle which regulates the existing social relations between the two sexes—the legal subordination of one sex to the other—is wrong in itself...and...ought to be replaced by a principle of perfect equality...[16]

---

[15] From *A Treatise on Education*, reprinted in *Sexual Politics*, by Kate Millet, p. 74.
[16] John Stuart Mill and Harriet Taylor Mill, *Essays on Sex Equality*, p. 125.

As a result of the Married Women's Property Act of 1870 and a series of other measures, wives in Britain were finally granted the right to own property. In 1919 British women were allowed to run for Parliament, and in 1928 they won the right to vote.

Suffrage Movement in America: Voting Rights

Women in the United States had received the vote in 1920—one of the results of a suffrage movement which began in July 1848 at the Women's Rights Convention at Seneca Falls, N.Y. The Declaration of Principles which Elizabeth Cady Stanton read at that meeting was broad in scope and more than a claim for the franchise. Paraphrasing the Declaration of Independence, it held "these truths to be self-evident; that all men and women are created equal." The Declaration of Principles itemized women's grievances and pledged to fight to attain the goal of equality. A resolution calling for women's suffrage carried by a small margin.

Early crusaders for women's rights in America often were active in the anti-slavery movement. "It was in the abolition movement that women first learned to organize, to hold public meetings, to conduct petition campaigns. As abolitionists they first won the right to speak in public, and they began to evolve a philosophy of their own place in society and of their basic rights. For a quarter of a century, the two movements, to free the slave and liberate the woman, nourished and strengthened one another."[17]

However, the women who had worked for the Negro's freedom and enfranchisement were bitterly disappointed with the 15th Amendment to the Constitution. The amendment, ratified in 1870, gave black men the right to vote but not women, either black or white. In an attempt to rally the discouraged suffragists, two organizations—the National Woman Suffrage Association and the American Woman Suffrage Association—were formed in 1869. The former, headed by Elizabeth Cady Stanton and Susan B. Anthony, worked for a constitutional amendment to enfranchise women; the latter, led by Lucy Stone and Julia Ward Howe, concentrated on a state-by-state approach.

After 1870, both groups tended to reject the more radical appeals for full equality and give priority to the suffrage issue. The two organizations came together as the National American Woman Suffrage Association in 1890. United or separate, neither had much tangible success in the 19th century. By 1900, only four states had granted women the franchise.[18] Suffrage

---

[17] Eleanor Flexner, *Century of Struggle: The Women's Rights Movement in the United States* (1959), p. 41.

[18] Wyoming, Colorado, Utah and Idaho.

was not to be won for 20 more years. That came on Aug. 26, 1920, when Secretary of State Bainbridge Colby proclaimed the 19th Amendment in effect. It stated: "The right of citizens of the United States to vote shall not be denied or abridged...on account of sex."

Influence of Books by de Beauvoir and Friedan

A later milestone in the history of modern feminism was the publication of *The Second Sex*, a scholarly and comprehensive study of the role of women in the past and present by Simone de Beauvoir. This book, which first appeared in translation in the United States in 1952, three years after its publication in France, became a best-seller. The value of de Beauvoir's book to feminist consciousness was that it covered virtually every aspect of the woman question and provided an encyclopedia of scholarship to be mined by future feminist writers. The general tone of the work was one of regret for women's limited opportunities for fulfillment as human beings. It looked forward to a time when men and women, without denying their differences, could function as true equals. The book's last chapter was entitled "Toward Liberation."

The next major book to influence the feminist movement was *The Feminine Mystique*, written in 1963 by Betty Friedan, an American. Friedan called on women to escape from what she considered the deadening enclosure of suburban domesticity and to seek a more fulfilling life as human beings. No longer, she wrote, did women need to be servants to the needs of others. Although she did not decry the roles of wife and mother, she contended that in modern times such roles were too narrow for healthy, intelligent women. Like de Beauvoir before her, Friedan attacked the Freudian view that a woman is so psychologically subject to her sexual and reproductive functions that she is destined to play a passive and retiring sex-determined role. Also, like de Beauvoir, she deplored the conditioning of women, from childhood on, to accept passive roles and depend on male leadership.

Friedan's book had a direct impact on the consciousness of American women who were susceptible to its message. Postwar brides with children now reaching adolescence were no longer devoted to simple domesticity; their daughters or younger sisters in college were becoming involved in movements that called for more personal self-expression in defiance of social custom. Both the housewives who stayed home and those who returned to work felt the sting of the Friedan message. Stirred by the interest in her book, Betty Friedan and others founded the National Organization for Women (Now) in 1966 to serve as an activist group for bringing pressure on government, industry and other organizations to end sex discrimination. NOW's statement of purpose presented a classic feminist position, along with a relatively conservative platform. It did not call for radical change in the performance of women's traditional functions, and it welcomed men as partners in reform.

A great deal of feminist activity has been concentrated in the United States since the 1960s. Numerous women's organizations have sprung up since the founding of NOW, such as the Women's Equity Action League and Women United, a group which has worked to promote an Equal Rights Amendment to the Constitution *(see p. 137)*. Although they are by no means united in their views, American women have been at the forefront of the modern feminist movement. It was not surprising, therefore, that a group of women from the United States, as members of the U.N. Commission on the Status of Women, was instrumental in instigating this year's international conference on women.

Prospects for Women Internationally

IN CONNECTION with this year's women's conference, the United Nations is urging member nations to ratify existing international treaties relating to women's rights. These include:

Convention on Equal Remuneration for Men and Women Workers for Work of Equal Value. Adopted by the ILO in 1951, it promotes the principle of equal pay for men and women for work of equal value. The principle may be applied by national laws or regulations, or collective agreements between employers and workers.

Convention on the Political Rights of Women. It was adopted by the U.N. General Assembly in 1952 to ensure women the right to vote, to be eligible for election, and to participate in public functions on equal terms with men.

Convention on the Nationality of Married Women. Under this treaty, approved by the General Assembly in 1957, marriage to an alien does not automatically affect the nationality of the wife.

Convention on Discrimination in Employment and Occupation. As adopted by the ILO in 1958, it calls for equality of opportunity and treatment in employment.

UNESCO[19] *Convention Against Discrimination in Education* (1960).

In addition, plans are under way to transform the Declaration on the Elimination of Discrimination Against Women (1967) into a treaty binding on governments.

[19] United Nations Educational, Scientific and Cultural Organization.

Despite its sponsorship of International Women's Year, the United Nations has been criticized for hiring and job promotion policies in its own offices that are said to discriminate against women. "The United Nations is made up of 138 countries in which women hold very few high policy positions," Dr. Ruth Bacon, director of the U.S. Center for International Women's Year, has said. "The position of women in the U.N. organization is a reflection of that fact."

"It would be the essence of hypocrisy if the U.N. Conference for International Women's Year were convened in 1975 without prior action by the United Nations to put its own house in order," Sen. Charles H. Percy (R Ill.) told the social affairs committee of the General Assembly as a U.N. representative in October 1974. "The U.N. should realize," Percy said, "that, as an institution, it has not lived up to the basic charter, which expresses...equal rights of men and women."[20]

"To create more paid jobs for women is the surest way simultaneously to raise their status, to reduce their drudgery, and to raise the national output."

Sir Arthur Lewis, *The Theory of Economic Growth*

At a congressional symposium on International Women's Year held in Washington, D.C., on May 14, 1975, Rep. Elizabeth Holtzman (D N.Y.) noted that all 19 of the Undersecretaries General at the United Nations were male. Of the 16 Assistant Secretaries General, only one is a woman. She is Helvi Sipila, Assistant Secretary-General for social development and humanitarian affairs, who now additionally serves as Secretary-General for International Women's Year. Rep. Holtzman also stated that fewer than 16 per cent of the 11,000 professional employees at the United Nations were women, while women made up 55 per cent of the non-professional staff. Male employees, she noted, received greater travel and pension benefits for their spouses than women employees did.[21] "The

---

[20] Quoted in *The Oregonian*, Oct. 25, 1974.
[21] For more details on the status of women in the United Nations, see "People in Glass Houses," by Pauline Frederick Robbins in *Ms.*, January 1975.

foolery and botching of the United Nations Secretariat will be taken as evidence that there is no public concern for the plight of women," feminist author Germaine Greer wrote in *The New York Times*, May 9, 1975. The International Women's Year conference, she predicted, would amount to little more than "hours of chatter."

When the United Nations approved International Women's Year in 1972, it voted no money for the project and did not provide for a world conference. It was only at the insistence of the U.N. Commission on the Status of Women, led by the United States and nine other countries, that an international meeting was finally scheduled. In 1974 the United Nations budgeted $258,000 for the Year, which includes the main conference and six regional meetings. Fewer than half of the U.N. member nations have endorsed a declaration of support for International Women's Year, and only 18 have contributed money to a voluntary fund which now totals approximately $1.2 million plus $500,000 from a private donation. In comparison, the World Population Conference spent $3.5 million.

U.S. Role in Women's Year; Status of the ERA

The United States, which officially donated $100,000 to the conference, has been active in promoting International Women's Year. The U.S. Center for International Women's Year was opened in September 1973 with a small grant from the Department of State. The Center does not lobby, but it distributes information on Women's Year and coordinates governmental and voluntary observances in connection with the Year. Ruth Bacon, director of the Center, reported great interest expressed by groups around the country and a mailing list which had grown from 400 to 8,000 names.

On Jan. 9, 1975, President Ford officially created a National Commission on the Observance of International Women's Year, but he did not appoint commissioners until April 2. Jill Ruckelshaus, a former White House director of women's affairs, was named chairperson, along with 38 other members, including Clare Boothe Luce, Katherine Hepburn, Alan Alda and Barbara Walters. The commission is scheduled to present its final report to the President by January 1976. Many hope the new group will be as influential as the Commission on the Status of Women, headed by Eleanor Roosevelt in the early 1960s, which stimulated interest in women's issues. Two congresswomen, Bella Abzug (D N.Y.) and Patsy Mink (D Hawaii), already have introduced bills calling for a White House conference on women. There has also been talk about the creation of a Cabinet-level department on women's issues.

Status of American Women

Education		Employment
Degree holders who are female.		Four out of 10 workers are women.
High school diplomas	51%	Women earn $3 for every $5 earned by men with similar jobs.
Bachelor's degrees	40	Only 14 per cent of women workers are in professional or technical fields.
Master's Degrees	34	
Doctoral degrees	12	Male high school graduates earn as much as women with five years or more of college.

SOURCE: *ZPG National Reporter*, January-February 1975.

The new National Commission on the Observance of International Women's Year will be concerned with the enforcement of anti-discrimination laws in employment, education and federal pension programs, but high on its list of considerations will be ratification of the Equal Rights Amendment. The proposed constitutional amendment to prohibit discrimination on the basis of sex has been approved by 32 of the 38 states required for ratification. The deadline is 1979. Twelve states have turned down the measure since January 1975. Seven of those were states which ERA supporters thought would vote to ratify.

One of the most vocal opponents is author Phyllis Schlafly, who is leading a "Stop ERA" campaign across the country. Schlafly and her followers believe that the amendment will lessen the dignity of the family and take away some of the privileged rights women now enjoy. One of her most persuasive arguments this year has been the contention that if the ERA became law, women would be forced to serve in the armed forces. ERA supporters counter that the draft law has expired. Barbara J. Katz has argued that even if it were reinstated, it is unlikely that a sizable part of the female population would be drafted. Only 7 per cent of eligible males were drafted during the peak of the Vietnam War, she has noted. Moreover, if husbands and fathers can be given deferrals, as they have in the past, so can wives and mothers.

ERA opponents also argue that the amendment would destroy labor laws described as protective of women. Proponents say the benefits of such laws are now being extended to cover both men and women. Other arguments against the amendment maintain that it would outlaw separate public restrooms for men and women; that it would deny wives the right to financial support; that it would affect personal relationships between men and women; and that it really isn't needed since women are already guaranteed equal rights under the Constitution. "You'll introduce chaos into the legal field if this amendment passes," former Sen. Sam J. Ervin Jr. (D N.C.) has said.[22]

Despite the "Stop ERA" campaign, a Gallup poll taken in March 1975 showed that six out of 10 Americans interviewed supported the ERA. In addition, a Louis Harris survey conducted in April 1975 showed that 51 per cent of the respondents favored passage, and that 59 per cent favored "efforts to strengthen and change women's status in society." Although frustrated in their efforts to ratify the amendment, ERA advocates are happy about the November 1974 elections. A record number of 18 women were elected to the House of Representatives, including all 12 incumbents who sought re-election. In addition, Ella T. Grasso was elected governor of Connecticut and Mary Anne Krupsak lieutenant governor of New York. Susie Sharp was elected chief justice of the supreme court in North Carolina, one of the states which recently rejected the ERA.

The gains were more impressive in state legislatures. According to the National Women's Political Caucus, 130 women were added to the state legislatures after the 1974 elections to bring the total to 600—almost double the 305 women legislators in office five years earlier. More significantly, perhaps, 1,207 women ran in state legislative races last year, up from 917 in 1972.

Rise of Feminist Concerns in Other Countries

Women's issues are very much a part of the political scene in the United States today. It is difficult to know, however, exactly how much importance other countries place on ending discrimination against women. According to the United Nations, the governments of Canada, Indonesia, Colombia, India and Sweden have within the past seven years established national commissions, advisory groups, special secretariats or councils to work for the advancement of women. In West Germany, university researchers and national statistical offices are beginning to devote more attention to gathering data on the contribution of women to society. Particularly in Europe and Latin America, women's bureaus affiliated with national ministries are attempting to improve employment opportunities and working conditions for women. In 1971 the Arab League countries established the Arab Commission on Women, and just recently a National Commission on Women's Employment Problems was formed in Italy.

---

[22] Quoted in *The New York Times*, March 20, 1975.

Wage Comparisons in Manufacturing

(Average women's earnings as a percentage of men's)

Country	1963	1972	1963-72
Australia	69.8	76.1	+ 6.3
Belgium	60.3	64.4	+ 4.1
Denmark	68.6	77.9	+ 9.3
Finland	66.6	71.3	+ 4.7
West Germany	68.7	70.7	+ 2.0
Ireland	57.2	57.2	0
Japan	44.2	47.5	+ 3.3
Sweden	72.1	83.2	+11.1
Switzerland	62.7	64.7	+ 2.0
United Kingdom	57.2	59.3	+ 2.1

SOURCE: *ILO Yearbook of Labour Statistics, 1973.*

In July 1974, President Giscard d'Estaing of France named Francoise Giroud, a magazine editor and supporter of women's rights, to head a new junior cabinet post of Secretary of State for the Status of Women. Last fall, in announcing her program, she revealed plans for spot announcements on television alerting women to their rights, and for posting notices in universities and factories as to where birth-control devices could be obtained.

When France enacted a law last summer making centraceptives readily available, it was estimated that only 10 per cent of the French women of child-bearing age had access to effective methods of contraception. France also ended a 54-year ban on abortion when, last fall, Minister of Health Simone Veil steered through the National Assembly a bill legalizing abortion during the first 10 weeks of pregnancy. According to Francoise Giroud, there is no strong feminist movement in France, "just something in the atmosphere."[23]

Several examples indicate that feminine consciences are being raised in other countries as well. Last year, several women's groups in Malaysia became so insulted over King Abdul Halim Shah's plans to take a teen-age beauty for his second wife that about 300 activists stormed the office of the prime minister and demanded that plans for the marriage be cancelled. Islam, the state religion, allows each man to have four wives.

In Japan last year, a group of women in steel helmets stormed an office on the 20th floor of the Kasumigaseki Tower in protest of an employee who had decided to leave his 40-year-old wife for

---

[23] Quoted in *The Christian Science Monitor*, Nov. 8, 1974.

a much younger woman. And in Poland, when 700 girls participating in a contest were asked "Would you like your husband
to have the same relation to you as your father has to your
mother?" More than half answered "no."

Outlook for Women's Conference in Mexico City

No one can readily predict what will happen when men and
women with varying interests and backgrounds converge in Mexico City to discuss the international problems of women. Among
some, there is the fear that a split may develop between women
from the advanced industrial countries and those from the
lesser-developed countries. Women from the "Third World"
countries of Asia, Africa and Latin America, for example, may
have trouble relating to western women's demands for more
career opportunities. It is likely that they will be more concerned with issues more vital to their needs, such as better
health care.

Other ideological differences may exist as well. "Man-the-
barricade rhetoric does turn off some women who attach a
great deal of importance to family life and to their role as
mothers," said Ruth Bacon. "And when they hear the word
'liberation' they think of revolutionary women in the streets
with guns. We have to be careful of the type of language we use."

---

*"Anyone with any knowledge of history
also knows that no great social upheavals
are possible without female ferment."*

Karl Marx

The New York Times reported June 4 that, according to
private American women's groups, the United Nations has been
trying to discourage activist organizations from attending the
Mexico City conference. It was estimated that more than 1,500
women were expected to attend a meeting of private groups to be
held apart from the official conference. *The Times* reported that
feminist leader Betty Friedan saw no conflict between western
women and Third World women because "we are our sister's
keeper." However, Carol Leimas of the American Association of
University Women has described the possibility of polarization:
"The Third World women fear that there will be an invasion of
American feminists in Mexico City this summer who will

Women and Education*

Country	Females over 15 who are literate	Females enrolled in school		
		Primary (age 6-11)	Secondary (age 12-17)	Higher (age 18-29)
Africa	16%	37%	20%	1%
Asia	43	54	24	2
Europe and Russia	95	90	83	11
Latin America	73	73	47	7
North America	98	99	95	19
Oceania	88	91	68	6

*Statistics for 1970.

SOURCE: *The* UNESCO *Courier*, March 1975.

---

dominate and raise issues not relevant to the Third World. And the Americans fear that the Third World women will concentrate only on the new economic order and forget the women's issues."[24]

The "new economic order" is a reference to a declaration of principles approved at a U.N. General Assembly special session on raw materials in 1974. The Assembly called for a redistribution of the world's wealth and material resources. Some persons are afraid that delegates to Mexico City from the developing countries will concentrate on promoting these principles and pay little attention to improving the position of women.

Proponents of the new economic order, including Mexican President Luis Echeverria Alvarez, have put forward the theory that after the world's resources are restructured, women in developing countries will automatically rise in status after they receive their share of the new wealth. Feminist leaders in the West disagree; they fear that economic development will continue to favor men.

---

[24] Quoted in *The New York Times*, March 3, 1975.

Selected Bibliography

Books

Boserup, Ester, *Women's Role in Economic Development*, St. Martin's Press, 1970.

de Beauvoir, Simone, *The Second Sex*, translated by H.M. Parshley, Knopf, 1953.

Friedan, Betty, *The Feminine Mystique*, Norton, 1963.

Galenson, Marjorie, *Women and Work: An International Comparison*, Cornell University, 1973.

Mill, John Stuart and Harriet Taylor Mill, *Essays on Sex Equality*, edited by Alice S. Rossi, The University of Chicago Press, 1970.

Millet, Kate, *Sexual Politics*, Doubleday & Company, 1970.

Notable American Women, 1607-1950: A Biographical Dictionary, James, E.T., et al. (eds.), Harvard University Press, 1971.

O'Neill, William L., *The Woman Movement: Feminism in the United States and England*, George Allen & Unwin, 1969.

Pescatello, Ann, editor, *Female and Male in Latin America: Essays*, University of Pittsburgh Press, 1973.

Articles

"International Women's Year," *Cooperation Canada*, January-February 1975, entire issue.

"International Women's Year," *The* UNESCO *Courier*, March 1975, entire issue.

Ms., January 1975, contains 10 articles relating to International Women's Year.

"Third World Woman," UNICEF *News*, July 1973, entire issue.

"Women and Development," UNICEF *News*, Issue 82/1974/4, entire issue.

"Women Around the World," *The Center Magazine*, May-June 1974.

Studies and Reports

Editorial Research Reports, "Status of Women," 1970 Vol. II, p. 565; "Women Voters," 1972 Vol. II, p. 765; "Women's Consciousness Raising," 1973 Vol. II, p. 497.

Food and Agriculture Organization of the United Nations, "The Role of Women in Rural Development," United Nations World Conference of the International Women's Year, E/CONF. 66/BP/11 March 24, 1975.

International Labor Organization, "Equality of Opportunity and Treatment for Women Workers," International Labor Conference 1975.

The Victor-Bostrom Fund for the International Planned Parenthood Federation, "Family Planning: Improving Opportunities for Women," Report No. 18, spring 1974.

United Nations Economic and Social Council, Report of the Special Rapporteur, "Study on the Interrelationship of the Status of Women and Family Planning," E/CN. 6/575, Nov. 27, 1973.

CHILD SUPPORT

by

Helen B. Schaffer

**Jan. 25
1 9 7 4**

CHILD SUPPORT

IN A NATION where more and more children are growing up in broken homes or are being raised in homes where they have never known more than one parent, the question of who shall support the children and how well should they be supported becomes of overwhelming public interest. Much of the spotlight falls on absentee fathers who evade the fundamental responsibility of parenthood. Pressure is now being brought to bear on these fathers from two sources. One is from a toughening of government policy on welfare cases in which the children's fathers have deserted their families. The other is from the demands of women's groups for stricter child-support orders and enforcement in divorce cases.

The fatherless family with small children is the focus of these crusades. Such families constitute an economically deprived group in the population, whether or not they receive assistance from the public purse. The women's rights groups seek to improve the economic position of one-parent families not only by extracting a larger financial contribution from the absentee parent, but by removing obstacles to the working mother's ability to earn a decent living.

Proposals to assure adequate financial support for the nation's children run into many controversies. The central issue concerns the extent to which society must or should take on a responsibility of this kind—that is, where to draw the line between the responsibilities of government and those of the family in providing the necessities of life for children. While government authorities emphasize a concern over "welfare cheating" or parental evasion of responsibility, other groups sympathetic to the interests of the poor point to the meagerness of assistance payments to the destitute. A government survey in 1972 showed that in 37 states the payments to families with dependent children did not meet basic family needs—as determined by the states' standards of assistance.

The movement for "no-fault" divorce[1] has aroused an opposition that contends such divorce laws will encourage pa-

---
[1] See "No-Fault Divorce," *E.R.R.*, 1973 Vol. II, pp. 779-798.

ternal desertion of responsibilities and throw even more rejected wives and their children on public assistance. There is controversy, too, over what the impact of the Equal Rights Amendment will have on child support if it is ratified. Proponents are now mounting a campaign to discredit the claims of its foes that the amendment would weaken the obligations of men to support their families. Other issues arise over needy children born out of wedlock.[2] There is dispute over the wisdom of pursuing "drifter" fathers whose earning power is meager. And there is disagreement as to whether federal enforcement machinery should be put to work collecting from fathers who cross state lines to evade court-issued support orders.

Pending Action in Congress for Enforcement

A bill pending in Congress would require states and localities to make a vigorous effort to track down absentee fathers of children on public assistance and make them pay for their children's support.[3] Sen. Russell B. Long (D La.), chairman of the Senate Finance Committee, has taken the lead for several years in promoting legislation of this kind. Under the pending measure, each state would establish a special unit responsible for obtaining support from absent parents of children receiving assistance under the AFDC (Aid to Families With Dependent Children) program.

The unit's functions would include (1) searching for the missing parent, (2) establishing paternity if the child was born out of wedlock, and (3) bringing action to obtain voluntary or compulsory contributions to the support of the children. The states could set up the new units in their departments of public welfare, but they would not be required to do so. In any event, the emphasis would be on collection rather than on social casework.

As many divorced, separated, or deserted mothers of small children can attest, a basic problem has been the ease with which the father moves to another state to evade a support order. The machinery for reciprocity is available, for all states have adopted some version of the model Reciprocal Enforcement of Support Act, drawn up by the National Conference of Commissioners on Uniform State Laws. But in

---

[2] A survey conducted by the Department of Health, Education, and Welfare in 1971 showed that 43.5 per cent of the families receiving Aid to Families with Dependent Children (then totaling 2,523,900 families) had at least one recipient child born out of wedlock.

[3] The provision was added by the Senate as an amendment to a bill (H.R. 3153) previously passed by the House in 1973. A House-Senate conference committee is expected to decide early in the 1974 session of Congress whether to retain the amendment. The bill itself deals with technical changes in the Social Security system.

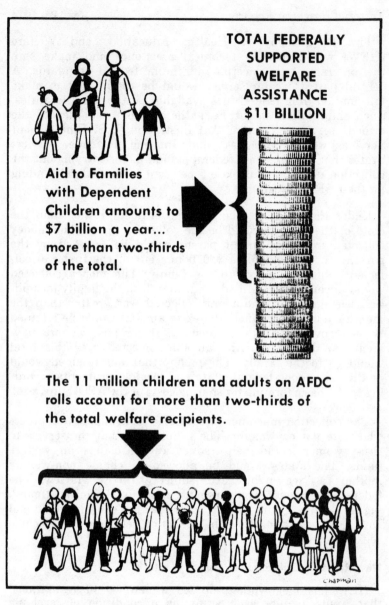

TOTAL FEDERALLY SUPPORTED WELFARE ASSISTANCE $11 BILLION

Aid to Families with Dependent Children amounts to $7 billion a year... more than two-thirds of the total.

The 11 million children and adults on AFDC rolls account for more than two-thirds of the total welfare recipients.

practice, many officials show little interest in pressing support claims originating outside of their own state. The pending bill in Congress would seek to overcome this by requiring the new unit to enter into cooperative arrangements with law-enforcement officials and courts in other states and to take vigorous action on paternity and support petitions. The federal government would pay 75 per cent of the state costs of administering the program.

The Department of Health, Education, and Welfare (HEW) would provide technical assistance and make sure the programs were meeting minimum federal standards. A central parent locator service would be established to make information from federal files available to states and localities. Such information might be gathered from the files of the armed services, Veterans Administration, U.S. Employment Service, welfare agencies, and Internal Revenue Service. States that did not meet federal standards for carrying out the collection program could lose 5 per cent of the federal funding for their AFDC programs.

Under the proposed plan, the government rather than the child or the mother would be the collection agent. The money collected from the absent parent would be retained by the government—except for a $20 bonus out of the first $50 collected, which would go to the family. The money collected would offset payments made that month to the family for public assistance. If the amount collected was greater than the month's public assistance, the extra amount would be retained by the government to compensate it for past welfare payments to the family. Any amount collected over this total would go to the family. The money that was retained would be divided among federal, state and local governments according to the basic formula for sharing costs of the AFDC program.

The collection machinery would also be available to mothers who were not on welfare. The rationale is that the service to these women could help reduce future claims on welfare funds. The states would be allowed to charge non-welfare mothers a "reasonable" fee, subject to HEW review. The federal government would provide much of the initial financing for setting up this service; after that the subsidy would end with the expectation that the collection service would become self-supporting.

New Rules on Children Born Out of Wedlock

HEW has meanwhile proposed a new set of regulations[4] that would require each state, as a condition of receiving federal AFDC funds, to establish the paternity of recipient children who are born out of wedlock and to make a strong effort to obtain support for them from the father or "any other legally liable person."

---

[4] The regulations, as approved by HEW Secretary Caspar W. Weinberger, were published in the Federal Register on Oct. 5, 1973; final adoption awaits the consideration of responses received from interested parties. The closing date for comments and objections was Nov. 5.

An official in HEW's Office of Policy Control told Editorial Research Reports that the department already had "changed" its approach to the AFDC problem and was now "actively encouraging" the states to pursue parents who wilfully shunt responsiblity for the support of their children onto the state. It was not so much a change of formal rules, he said, as a "change of posture." The department was letting welfare officials in the states know that technical help on the problem was available to them. HEW Secretary Caspar W. Weinberger told the Senate Finance Committee on Sept. 25, 1973, that it had become the department's policy to urge all states to "follow the example" set by those states that had recently intensified their efforts in that direction. He mentioned California and Washington as good models.

Reduction of Cases in California and Michigan

California's crackdown on negligent fathers dates from enactment of the state Welfare Reform Act in 1971. A "critical element" of the new law, according to Ronald A. Zumbrun of the Pacific Legal Foundation, was "to convince county authorities and the public that enforcing child support obligations is a law-enforcement function rather than social casework." The Reform Act gave district attorneys authority to demand immediate referral of all absent-father welfare cases to them, "thus placing full responsibility for child support in the law-enforcement office." The act also offered the counties a financial incentive (37.25 per cent of collections) to go after the fathers. And the fathers, when apprehended, were faced with the choice of paying up or going to jail.

California officials reported a $1 billion saving in total welfare costs in two years, due to increased collections and a drop of 352,000 in the number of persons on welfare. As a result of lower costs, property taxes were cut in 42 counties and the state treasury accumulated an $850 million surplus which the 1973 session of the legislature returned to the taxpayers. The Family Responsibility Act, enacted in 1972 and effective March 7, 1973, made it easier to carry paternity and child-support actions across county lines, and it gave child-support collections priority over other debt collections.

Michigan, which instituted an intensive "runaway pappy" program under legislation enacted in 1971, reports that support collections rose from $11 million in 1970 to more than $28 million in 1972. The Michigan program provides for cooperative arrangements between the state and local units of government, with state funding for locating parents, establishing paternity, and enforcing child-support collections.

Local "father finders" staffs are especially trained for the job. William Meyer, deputy inspector general of the Michigan Department of Social Services, told the Senate Finance Committee that the program returned $3.30 for every $1.00 invested in it.

Call for Support Protection in Divorce Cases

Women's rights groups believe the general public does not fully appreciate the privations and injustices that afflict many divorcees with young children. They are particularly concerned over the spread of "no-fault" divorce laws. Twenty states now have laws in accordance with the principle of the Uniform Marriage and Divorce Act that permits a court to dissolve a marriage simply by a finding that the marriage is "irretrievably broken."[5] But most of the states that adopted the no-fault provision of the model act did not adopt other provisions which were designed to protect the support rights of the family.

Among these provisions was a requirement that the court, in setting the support payment, consider the standard of living the child previously enjoyed. The model law also would authorize the court to order that the amount of support be paid directly out of the father's wages from the beginning of the support period—rather than after he has become delinquent. Only six of the no-fault states—Arizona, California, Colorado, Kentucky, Missouri, and Washington—have adopted at least some of the support-protection features.

The Citizens' Advisory Council on the Status of Women, a presidentially appointed group,[6] adopted a resolution on Nov. 10, 1973, urging women's organizations to press for amendments in state divorce laws "to assure that the rights of homemakers and children are given just recognition." The resolution also recommends that state legislatures "review and revise their divorce laws adopting as a minimum the economic protections of the Uniform Marriage and Divorce Act." The council has said it does not oppose "no-fault" divorce in principle, but it has said that a husband who wants a divorce is likely to make relatively generous provisions for family support to win his wife's cooperation in states where the law re-

---

[5] The uniform act was promulgated in 1970 by the National Conference of Commissioners on Uniform State Laws. It was modeled on an earlier enactment in California. Nineteen states have since acted on the proposal. See "No-Fault Divorce," *E.R.R.*, 1973 Vol. II, pp. 779-796.

[6] Established by presidential executive order in 1963, its main function is "to suggest, to arouse public awareness...and to stimulate action with private and public institutions, organizations, and individuals working for improvement of conditions of special concern to women."

Family Income Distribution		
Family status	Children under 18 (in thousands)	Median family income, 1971
Total	65,255	$10,845
Husband-wife families	56,625	11,749
Female head of family	7,924	4,207
Mother in labor force	4,040	5,496
Mother not in labor force	3,884	3,229

SOURCE: Department of Labor, *Monthly Labor Review*, April 1973

quires that some fault be shown to justify a divorce. The rejected wife loses this leverage if her husband can obtain a divorce without her cooperation.

Payments for child support in divorce cases are believed to provide less than one-half the amount needed to support the children, the council said. A survey of judges conducted, in 1965 by the American Bar Association's Section on Family Law indicated that 60 per cent of the judges allotted one-third or less—sometimes much less—of the father's income for child support. "Most judgments for child support allow such minimal sums as $15...$25...[and] $30 a week," Adele Weaver, president of the National Association of Women Lawyers, told the House Judiciary Subcommittee in 1971 when it was considering the Equal Rights Amendment.

More generous support orders are not necessarily a solution because the orders are often not obeyed. Elizabeth C. Spalding of Greenwich, Conn., coordinator of a National Task Force on Marriage and Family Relations and Divorce, has spoken of the "myth" that women make money on divorce. "In fact," she told the Senate Finance Committee, "divorced women seldom get alimony...[and] child support orders are inadequate in amounts and almost impossible to collect."[7] Her organization is conducting a survey of the workload of the marital courts in a number of states. Evidence already collected indicates an enormously heavy load of support-enforcement cases, and many delays and failures in collections.

According to Ms. Spalding more women than in the past are relinquishing their right to custody of their children because

---

[7] Testimony on Sept. 25, 1973. Her organization was sponsored by the National Organization for Women (NOW).

they know the children will be better off financially if the father retains custody. In several recent cases, judges awarded custody of the children to the father and ordered the employed mother to contribute financially to the support of the children. This is hardly a trend, however. Mothers still get custody in the vast majority of cases. Many of them struggle to make ends meet and some land on public assistance.

Where the marriage is still legally intact, husbands in practically all states can be held criminally liable for non-support of wife and children. But the Status of Women Council reported that "most states require that the wife or children be in 'destitute or necessitous circumstances' or without sufficient or reasonable means of support." As in other criminal proceedings, guilt must be established beyond reasonable doubt and the burden of proof is on the state," the council reported. "The defendant is entitled to a jury trial. This type of statute is used extensively in welfare cases, mothers often being required to file complaints under criminal non-support statutes as a condition of receiving public assistance."[8]

Even when the husband remains a conscientious resident breadwinner, his wife is increasingly likely to be employed while the children are small. Thus whether the mother is the sole support of the family, supplements the father's wages, or is the child's agent in obtaining public assistance, the important sociological fact is that the American child is becoming more accustomed to regarding his mother as a major producer of the income that keeps the family afloat.

Historic View of the Dependent Child

FOR MUCH OF HISTORY, the child from an early age contributed significantly to his own and his family's support. The farm child has always been a valued economic asset to the family, so much so that in the early years of public education, school months were adapted to the seasonal needs for agricultural labor. Generally speaking, until recent centuries the child at about age seven became a part of the adult community, serving his elders, and learning from them as befitted the family's station in life.[9] In ancient and medieval times, this meant that most children were early put to arduous drudgery

---

[8] Citizens' Advisory Council on the Status of Women, *The Equal Rights Amendment and Alimony and Child Support Laws,* January 1972.

[9] See Phillipe Aries's *Centuries of Childhood* (1962).

in house and field. Under the medieval guild system, children were apprenticed to masters, in whose homes they lived and received support until ready for independent employment.

Until the industrial revolution, family income consisted less of cash than of goods and services produced cooperatively by family members. But with the coming of the factory, family support began to rely on cash wages, and the responsibility for earning those wages fell, in accordance with tradition, on the father. His wages, however, often were insufficient for family sustenance and the juveniles of the family were drawn into factory employment at even lower wage rates.

"From the beginning, the typical dependent-child family has been father-less."

As in England, child labor manned the textile mills of New England. Boys and girls aged 7 to 12 served in the first cotton mill, which began operating in Rhode Island in 1790. Later, entire families were hired under single wage agreements. Juvenile residents of almshouses provided still more cheap labor for textile mills. According to a report of 1832,[10] two-fifths of all employees of New England factories were aged 7 to 16; their hours were never less than 10, seldom less than 12, and often more.

Child labor in American mills increased in the late 19th century, then began to decline. But in some states it remained high. In Pennsylvania, for example, more than 11 per cent of all silk mill operatives in 1920 were under 16, A contemporary report told of 120,000 "little ones," some as young as seven, working at the turn of the century in the mines, mills, factories and "sweatshops" of Pennsylvania. In the United States as a whole, 24,000 children were said to be working at that time in dangerous occupations for long hours in and near mines and quarries.[11]

A crusade against oppressive child labor in the United States moved ahead slowly. The first child labor law in the country was adopted in Massachusetts in 1836. It provided that no child under 15 could be employed in manufacturing

---

[10] By the New England Association of Farmers, Mechanics, and Other Working Men.

[11] Robert Hunter, *Poverty* (1904), excerpt reprinted in *Poverty in the Affluent Society* (1966), pp. 17-18.

unless he had attended school for at least three months in the preceding year. By 1930 all but two states had established 14 as the minimum age for full-time employment in industry, but the rule did not apply to agriculture or domestic service where many children were employed.

The first federal law limiting child labor was adopted in 1916 but was declared unconstitutional by the Supreme Court two years later. A provision of a revenue act in 1919 imposed a tax on the profits of mining and manufacturing establishments that employed children but that act, too, was declared unconstitutional, in 1922. A constitutional amendment restricting child labor was approved by Congress in 1924 but failed to be ratified by the states. Finally, in 1938, Congress enacted the Fair Labor Standards Act. One of its provisions banned goods from interstate commerce that had been produced with the use of "oppressive child labor."[12] The constitutionality of the act was sustained by the Supreme Court in 1941.

Child labor is by no means absent on the American scene today but its declining significance is indicated by the fact that the U.S. Labor Department, in its statistical reporting on the labor force, began in 1967 to base its computations on the population beginning at age 17 rather than 14. The American value system still has a high regard for after-school jobs in certain types of employment. In middle-class families, such chores as newspaper delivery and baby sitting are considered character building, and the earnings are the child's own.[13]

Almshouses and Indenture for Pauper Children

"Dependent child" is a term that has come to denote a child who has no means of support except from the government or private charity. "The practice of charity, one of the roots of modern child welfare, ...reaches far back into history, particularly in the form of concern for orphans."[14] Greece at the time of Plato provided for the children of soldiers killed in battle. The Roman Empire made provisions for indigent children. In the early Christian era and throughout the Middle Ages, the church was the main source of sustenance for the needy. Destitute or abandoned children were taken into the care of religious orders in monasteries and convents or in orphan asylums and foundling hospitals run by the church.

---

[12] Defined as the general employment of children under 16—except for 14- and 15-year-olds with Department of Labor permission—and those under 19 in hazardous jobs.

[13] Employment of teen-agers, whether in or out of school, is increasing. See Kopp Michelotti, "Young Workers: In School and Out," *Monthly Labor Review,* September 1973, pp. 11-15.

[14] "Child," *Encyclopedia of Social Sciences* (1930), Vol. 13, p. 413.

When the manorial system, which offered some security to the poorest child, began to disintegrate, the number of wandering destitute persons of all ages began to grow. The English Poor Law of 1601 was the first to make direct provision from the government treasury for the poverty-stricken. Thus developed the earliest form of foster care for poor children— the indenturing of them to artisans or to families. The child paid for his keep by serving his master and at the end of his indenture period, at age 18 or older, he would be expected to pay whatever else was owed his benefactors out of future earnings.

Provisions for destitute children in the American colonies reflected the harsh attitudes that prevailed in England. "When young settlers were needed they were separated from parents in England and shipped to this country under indenture. In practically all the American colonies dependent children were indentured to families, thus delimiting public responsibility for them."[15] Charity was not absent but it was given intermittently, at the whim of the giver.

Institutions were founded in the 18th and 19th centuries, to shelter the destitute but parents in poverty were often required to relinquish custody of their children forever in order to secure shelter for them. The almshouse, which began to appear in the United States in mid-18th century, was regarded at first as a humane advancement. But criticism soon developed. Children were housed in the same institution with the destitute and infirm of all ages. A New York State legislative inquiry of 1856 denounced the "filth, nakedness, licentiousness, [and] general bad morals" in the almshouses, which were described as "the worst possible nurseries" for the young. Next came the founding of an institution solely for children, the orphanage, which was "acclaimed in the 19th century as a panacea...[and] regarded as a progressive step in child care."[16]

Rise and Fall of Tax-Funded Private Asylums

State responsibility for the care of indigent children during the 19th century increasingly took the form of providing public subsidies to privately operated—usually denominational— orphan asylums. The system was appealing because private charities were considered better suited than the state to the care of children, and the subsidy plan was less burdensome on the taxpayer than other forms of poor relief. Because subsidies

---

[15] Justine Wise Polier, *Everybody's Children, Nobody's Child* (1941), p. 8.
[16] *Ibid*, p. 14.

AFDC Families by Status of Father

	Per cent		Per cent
Father dead	4.3	Deserted	15.2
Incapacitated	9.8	Not married to	
Unemployed, employed		mother	27.7
part-time, or enrolled		In prison	2.1
in training program	6.1	Other reason	1.2
Divorced	14.2	Stepfather case	2.6
Legally separated	2.9	Mother absent	0.9
Separated without		Unknown	0.1
court decree	12.9		

were paid on a per capita basis, it was to the interest of the institution to take in all who applied for admission and to keep the children for a long time. In the absence of direct relief, parents of little means were sometimes induced to turn their children over to the institutional shelter. According to a study published in 1902, many parents, including immigrants, "came to regard the institutions somewhat in the light of free boarding schools."[17]

For many years the institutions were not subject to public supervision and they resisted the efforts of reformers to impose controls. Legislators were cautious not to offend religious groups that sponsored the asylums. In addition, there was a prevailing fear that putting private asylums under governmental control might subject them to the evils of the spoils system. Eventually, however, controls were applied. The institutions had come under criticism for over-regimentation and failure to appreciate the psychological needs of children. A critic, writing of conditions prior to World War I, said the institutions "meant closed walls, children segregated from the community, trained in separate schools, amenable to a stern quasi-military regime, commanded by the sound of the cowbell..."[18]

Usually, only the older children were placed for adoption and the procedure was closer to the indenture system than to the modern concept of adoption.[19] There was little investigation or follow-up by adoptive homes. A well-intentioned movement sought to "rescue" homeless newsboys and other near-destitute children in eastern cities from the evils of city streets and send them to live under healthier conditions with farm families in the West. It is estimated that 20,000 children

---

[17] Homer Folks, *The Care of Destitute and Delinquent Children.*
[18] Elias L. Trotzkey, *Institutional Care and Placing Out* (1930), cited by Polier, *op. cit.,* p. 15.
[19] See "Child Adoption," *E.R.R.*, 1973 Vol. I, pp. 479-496.

AID TO FAMILIES WITH DEPENDENT CHILDREN

Period	Families	Total recipients	Children	Per family	Per recipient	Payments (in thousands)
				Average monthly payment		
December:	— (in thousands) —					
1940	372	1,222	895	$ 32.40	$ 9.85	$ 133,393
1945	274	943	701	52.05	15.15	149.475
1950	651	2,233	1,661	71.45	20.85	547,174
1955	602	2,192	1,661	85.50	23.50	612,209
1960	803	3,073	2,370	108.35	28.35	994,425
1961	916	3,566	2,753	114.65	29.45	1,148,838
1962	932	3,789	2,844	119.10	29.30	1,289,824
1963	954	3,930	2,951	122.40	29.70	1,355,538
1964	1,012	4,219	3,170	131.30	31.50	1,496,525
1965	1,054	4,396	3,316	136.95	32.85	1,644,096
1966	1,127	4,666	3,526	150.10	36.25	1,849,886
1967	1,297	5,309	3,986	161.70	39.50	2,249,673
1968	1,522	6,086	4,555	168.15	42.05	2,823,841
1969	1,875	7,313	5,413	176.05	45.15	3,533,281
1970	2,552	9,659	7,033	187.95	49.65	4,852,964
1971	2,918	10,653	7,707	190.90	52.30	6,204,072
1972	3,122	11,065	7,984	191.20	53.95	6,908,373
1973 (May)	3,152	11,000	7,937	189.15	53.65	589,986

SOURCE: Social and Rehabilitation Service, Department of Health, Education, and Welfare.

"went West" in this movement between 1854 and 1875, but toward the end of the century the western states began to stop the movement or subject it to state regulation.

Institutionalization prevailed as a major means for the support of indigent children until well into the 20th century. The Census Bureau in 1933 recorded 243,000 known dependent and neglected children in the United States, of whom 58 per cent were in institutions. By this time, however, sentiment had grown in favor of keeping children in their own homes or in accredited foster homes where they could live as children of the family rather than as virtual indentured servants. This sentiment was furthered by the Depression Thirties, when the enormous increase in the number of families deprived of earnings produced a burden too big for private charity to handle.

New Deal's Introduction of Public Assistance

Emergency relief measures instituted early in the New Deal era provided cash, food, clothing and other necessities directly to families in need, including many families in which the father was unemployed. The emergency provisions were supplanted by programs instituted under the Social Security

Act of 1935; it provided insurance benefits for unemployed and retired workers and federal aid to states for direct relief to certain categories of individuals not in the labor market— the aged, the blind, and "dependent children."[20] These were children in families with no wage earner or with earnings too meager to provide the necessities of life.

From the beginning, the typical dependent-child family has been fatherless. In the early years death was the most frequent reason for the father's absence; today a deceased father is reported in fewer than 5 per cent of AFDC cases. One reason for the relative decline is that Social Security benefits are available to minor children of deceased or disabled workers. The original welfare act was based on the premise that it was better for fatherless children to remain at home with their mother than to be placed in an institution or with a sitter while she worked. The pressure now is on welfare mothers to make themselves at least partially self-supporting if the children are old enough to go to school.[21]

Child Support Problems and Proposals

AT FIRST GLANCE it might seem reasonable to expect that mothers of children in need would want to cooperate with authorities in locating and bringing legal pressure on absentee fathers to contribute to the children's support. But objections have been raised to provisions in some laws that make it obligatory for a woman to cooperate in this matter if she wants her children to remain eligible for assistance.[22]

Mrs. Kenneth Greenawalt of the League of Women Voters told the Senate Finance Committee during its 1973 hearings that such a provision contains "the potential for harassment... discriminates against AFDC recipients...and deepens the separation of people living in poverty." The woman might have reason to fear reprisal, possibly bodily harm, if she helped bring legal action against the father. There are also objections that mothers of out-of-wedlock children on relief be required to cooperate in the legal determination of paternity. Representatives of the Child Welfare League of America argued it would be detrimental to the interest of the

---

[20] Later the disabled were added to both insurance and public assistance programs.

[21] See "Child Care," *E.R.R.*, 1972 Vol. I, pp. 439-458.

[22] The laws provide that if the mother refused to cooperate, her needy children would receive funds through an agent other than the mother, but the mother would not be paid the amount she normally received as the children's caretaker—in effect, reducing total payment to the family.

AFDC DISTRIBUTION BY STATES, AUGUST 1973

State	Number of families	Number of recipients Total [1]	Children	Average money payment per recipient
Total	3,143,161	10,857,283	7,839,614	$54.71
Alabama	46,615	160,819	120,837	21.39
Alaska	3,974	11,585	8,660	70.57
Arizona	20,131	72,773	55,650	34.93
Arkansas	25,118	87,203	65,136	32.27
California	417,022	1,347,328	938,236	65.66
Colorado	29,428	96,150	70,097	55.07
Connecticut	34,584	116,603	86,186	71.11
Delaware	8,887	29,966	21,980	33.40
District of Columbia	30,031	102,905	75,112	61.52
Florida	87,542	304,881	231,249	30.75
Georgia	103,806	339,678	250,280	30.85
Guam	646	2,674	2,099	45.75
Hawaii	13,890	45,150	31,951	86.89
Idaho	5,749	19,140	13,497	53.93
Illinois	205,425	771,664	560,862	63.57
Indiana	49,584	170,265	125,349	40.52
Iowa	23,850	79,961	56,101	54.82
Kansas	21,865	69,936	52,525	59.51
Kentucky	45,753	155,452	110,570	36.30
Louisiana	69,525	257,610	194,767	25.20
Maine	20,278	70,562	49,767	39.52
Maryland	66,450	221,662	162,896	45.88
Massachusetts	88,925	301,420	217,840	73.70
Michigan	174,898	595,000	426,458	68.94
Minnesota	41,159	123,918	89,296	75.59
Mississippi	50,125	181,420	141,589	14.47
Missouri	72,480	240,255	178,761	31.03
Montana	6,737	20,892	15,554	47.37
Nebraska	11,791	39,338	28,939	44.57
Nevada	4,477	13,725	10,183	42.34
New Hampshire	7,308	23,412	16,614	69.55
New Jersey	118,394	419,996	303,512	71.67
New Mexico	17,706	60,101	44,771	36.51
New York	347,543	1,219,761	862,922	80.18
North Carolina	46,136	149,340	110,997	41.32
North Dakota	4,442	14,110	10,437	62.28
Ohio	140,662	485,765	349,194	45.92
Oklahoma	27,576	94,972	71,585	44.00
Oregon	25,026	77,248	53,478	65.25
Pennsylvania	168,394	615,540	425,978	63.32
Puerto Rico	52,023	258,561	190,239	9.22
Rhode Island	14,122	48,808	34,750	66.23
South Carolina	32,104	116,966	87,468	24.41
South Dakota	6,516	21,923	16,298	56.19
Tennessee	57,909	191,392	143,557	31.51
Texas	118,223	426,447	314,265	30.88
Utah	13,807	40,127	28,393	68.22
Vermont	5,560	19,205	13,137	68.02
Virgin Islands	928	3,567	2,895	36.48
Virginia	47,825	163,312	118,205	49.52
Washington	45,269	143,827	95,778	71.37
West Virginia	17,947	66,650	46,441	41.23
Wisconsin	44,770	139,278	101,043	76.89
Wyoming	2,226	7,040	5,230	48.86

[1] Includes the children and one or both parents or one caretaker relative other than a parent in families in which the requirements of such adults were considered in determining the amount of assistance.

SOURCE: *Social Security Bulletin*, January 1974

child to make a paternity determination in some situations—as in cases of incest, for example.

Another problem in out-of-wedlock cases is how to make a definitive judgment on paternity. "The chance of error—indeed the likelihood of error—if blood grouping tests are conducted inexpertly, makes it imperative that courts be warned not to accept blood typing evidence [in paternity cases] unless there is assurance that the tests have been conducted in accordance with the highest standards of care," Harry D. Krause wrote in *Illegitimacy: Law and Social Policy* (1971). Krause, a professor of law at the University of Illinois is currently engaged in a study of the status of blood testing for paternity determinations under a grant from the Office of Child Development.

Paternity Determinations; Wage Garnishment

Krause told the Senate Finance Committee that he believed it was feasible to establish regional laboratories for paternity determination, but "some changes in state laws of evidence probably will be required." The National Conference of Commissioners on Uniform State Laws in July 1973 approved a Uniform Parentage Act and sent it to the American Bar Association for consideration of endorsement. The bar association and the American Medical Association have a joint committee to investigate current and potential capabilities in this area.

Once the father is apprehended there is the question of how to make sure he will continue to make support payments regularly over the long term of his obligation. While the threat of imprisonment may induce a reluctant father to begin or resume payments, it may not prevent his subsequent disappearance, necessitating a new search and another round of enforcement procedures. For members of the armed forces and federal civilian employees, child-support obligations would be withheld from their pay, under terms of the pending bill in Congress.

Perhaps the most difficult problem in child-support cases is that of getting a large enough contribution from low-paid fathers, especially when they have established new families elsewhere. Mrs. Ben W. Heineman, president of the board of directors of the Child Welfare League of America, raised this question in her testimony before the Senate Finance Committee. "These are working fathers, and imposing burdens greater than they can afford may prove a disincentive to work, impose hardships, and discourage ultimate family stability," she said.

It has been observed that marital trouble originates because "there is not enough money coming into the household to run it."[23] Trying to stretch that income to support two separate households puts even more strain on the resources.

Question of Upgrading Family's Earning Power

Critics of the current effort to reduce the number of children on public assistance believe the effort should be a more broad-based one designed to raise the earning capacity of the family wage earner, whether it is the father or the mother who fills this role. The most recent survey of urban employment in six major cities confirmed the obvious: that "residents of slum areas in central cities have difficulty finding work, and when they do, they do not make much money." Two out of 10 were working part-time, one in 10 earned less than the official poverty level of income for a family of four ($3,900 in 1970 when the survey was made.[24]

A spokesman for the National Association of Social Workers and other service organizations[25] urged that the "runaway pappy" programs be conducted "in conjunction with effective family rehabilitation programs." Desertion, these groups asserted, "is mainly a low-income group circumstance," and "dealing with it only as a fiscal matter is a loser." Another group, the National Assembly for Social Policy and Development, said it was necessary to "recognize the practical social climate in which desertion occurs." The best way to deal with desertion was to "strengthen the underpinnings of society as a whole" through "an adequate range of jobs, education, housing, income, and opportunities for all."

Comparable groups continue to support some form of guaranteed income or family assistance plan. President Nixon first proposed a family assistance plan in 1969, but later dropped it when the issue became rent with controversy in Congress.[26] The Nixon administration is reported to be preparing a new plan. Despite the intense debate that the past proposals have generated, the outcome of debate in the early 1970s left proponents in doubt whether guaranteed income was an idea whose time had yet come.

---

[23] Section on Family Law, American Bar Association, "What Are Our Domestic Relations Judges Thinking?" (Monograph No. 1), July 1965.

[24] Daniel S. Whipple, "Employment Among the Poor of Six Central Cities," *Monthly Labor Review*, October 1973, p. 52. The six cities were Atlanta, Chicago, Detroit, Houston, Los Angeles, and New York.

[25] The American Association of Psychiatric Services for Children, National Conference of Catholic Charities, National Council of Jewish Women, and the National Urban League. Their views were presented in a statement to the Senate Finance Committee, Sept. 27, 1973.

[26] See *Congress and the Nation* (1973), Vol. III, pp. 622-627.

Selected Bibliography

Books

Burgess, M. Elaine, and Daniel O. Price, *An American Dependency Challenge*, American Public Welfare Association, 1963.

Congress and the Nation, Vol. III, Congressional Quarterly, 1973.

Goodwin, Leonard, *Do the Poor Want to Work?* The Brookings Institution, 1972.

Kriesberg, Louis, *Mothers in Poverty*, Aldine Publishing Co., 1970.

Meissner, Hanna H., ed., *Poverty in the Affluent Society*, Harper & Row, 1966.

Milwaukee County Welfare Rights Organization, *Welfare Mothers Speak Out*, W. W. Norton and Co., 1972.

Moynihan, Daniel P., *The Politics of Guaranteed Income*, Random House, 1973.

Vadakin, James C., *Children, Poverty, and Family Allowances*, Basic Books, 1968.

Articles

"Child Support in Missouri: The Father's Duty, the Child's Right, and the Mother's Ability to Enforce," *Missouri Law Review*, summer 1971.

Diaz, Capt. Robert E., "Pursuing the Elusive Nonsupporting Serviceman," *JAG* [Judge Advocate General] *Law Review*, May 1973.

Hayghe, Howard, "Labor Force Activity of Married Women," *Monthly Labor Review*, April 1973.

"Lightening the Welfare Load" (interview with Robert B. Carleson, special assistant for welfare to the secretary of health, education and welfare), *Nation's Business*, August 1973.

Michelotti, Kopp, "Young Workers: In School and Out," *Monthly Labor Review*, September 1973.

Young, Anne M., "Children of Working Mothers," *Monthly Labor Review*, April 1973.

Studies and Reports

American Bar Association Section on Family Law, "What Are Our Domestic Relations Judges Thinking?" (Monograph No. 1), July 1965.

Citizens Advisory Council on the Status of Women, *"The Equal Rights Amendment and Alimony and Child Support Laws"* (memorandum), January 1972.

Editorial Research Reports, "Child Care," 1972 Vol. I, pp. 439-458; "Child Adoption," 1973 Vol. I, pp. 477-496.

National Center for Social Statistics, *Public Assistance Programs: Standards for Basic Needs*, May 14, 1973.

Senate Committee on Finance, *Child Support and the Work Bonus* (hearing held Sept. 25, 1973), U.S. Government Printing Office, 1973, Stock Number 5270-02021.

"Senator Mondale's Study of the State of the American Family," *Congressional Record*, Oct. 1, 1973, pp. S 18183-S 18200.

INDEX

P

Parents. *See also* Single-parent Families
    Changing attitudes toward child-rearing - 6
    Child care, housekeeping roles - 6
    Diminishing influence on teenagers - 10
    Need for flexible work schedules - 17, 79
    "New-breed" - 7
    Self-fulfillment - 6-8, 133
Parents Without Partners (PWP) - 70, 81
Paternity determinations. *See* Absentee Fathers
Pay. *See* Income
Philadelphia Plan - 54
Plato, *The Republic* - 130
Polls, Opinion
    Abortion issue - 107, 108, 111, 118
    Attitudes toward child-rearing - 7
    Attitudes toward working wives - 26, 34
    ERA - 138
Political rights. *See* Suffrage
Population control. *See* Family Planning
Porter, Sylvia - 24
Preferential treatment. *See* Affirmative Action
Pregnancy pay - 39
Project on Equal Education Rights (PEER) - 92, 93
Property rights - 13, 129, 130, 132
Protests. *See also* Feminist Movement
    Abolition - 132
    Abortion reform - 112
    Pregnancy pay benefits - 39
    Right-to-life movement - 117, 118
    'Stop ERA' - 137
    Suffrage - 132
    Women's sports movement - 93
    Workingwomen's reforms - 32, 131

R

Reverse Discrimination. *See also* Affirmative Action
    AT&T cases - 37, 47, 58
    Philadelphia Plan controversy - 54
    Preferential treatment (pro-con) - 48-49
    Suits by white males - 46
    Supreme Court rulings - 46, 55, 59
Representation

Proposed Cabinet Office of women's issues - 136
    Rise of Liberalism - 131
    Suffrage movements - 13, 32, 131, 132
Roosevelt, Eleanor - 136
Rosellini, Lynn - 101
Rousseau, Jean Jacques - 131

S

Scannel, Nancy - 101
Schlafly, Phyllis - 137
Seniority rights - 58
Sex-role Stereotyping. *See also* Careers
    Liberalization of courtship and sex mores - 13
    Myths about women athletes - 86, 87
    Occupational segregation - 28
    Patriarchal supremacy - 12, 129
    Psychic barriers to women's advancement - 40
    Public opinion. *See* Polls, Opinion
    Secretary traps - 27, 41
    Womanhood as a vocation - 13, 32, 133, 140
Single-parent Families. *See also* Parents
    American families (1975) - 69
    Bachelor fathers - 78
    Changing family patterns - 3, 71
    Child-adoption increase - 67, 78
    Child care problems - 71, 79
    Child support decrees. *See* Child Support
    Concern for children in family disorganization - 74
    Economic handicaps - 68, 76, 79
    Emotional and social issues, 70, 74-75
    Information clearinghouses - 81
    Joint custody arrangements - 80
    Male-headed - 69, 78
    Mean family income (1974) - 76
    Median incomes (1975) - 70
    Public policy implications - 75
    Welfare income - 70, 76, 77, 156
Sipila, Helvi - 126, 127, 128, 135
Social Security
    Emergency aid to families - 157, 158
    Proposed Income-support systems - 17
Spalding, Elizabeth C. - 151
Sports. *See* Careers, Athletic
Stanton, Elizabeth Cady - 132
Suffrage Movements
    British reform movement - 131
    Prospects for women internationally - 134
    Suffrage movement in America - 13, 32, 132